Life IN THE
CAMEL
LANE

EMBRACE THE ADVENTURE

DOREEN M. CUMBERFORD

Life in the Camel Lane: Embrace the Adventure
Published by White Heather Press
Denver, CO

ISBN: 978-0-578-60735-1
TRAVEL / Special Interest / Adventure
Cover and Interior design by Victoria Wolf, Wolf Design and Marketing

QUANTITY PURCHASES: Schools, companies, professional groups, clubs, and other organizations may qualify for special terms when ordering quantities of this title. For information, email doreencp@gmail.com.

White Heather
PRESS

For the women who went to Saudi
Arabia over the last eight decades,
in commemoration of the stamina with
which they pursued adventure.

Contents

PART 3 LIMINAL LIVING

PART 4 NEW PARADIGMS

PART FIVE RE-ENTRY

FINALE

في يوم من الأيام

I Am From

I am from Scotland, Cameroon, Dubai and now California sun.

I am from history, geography and embracing all that I can.

I am from peach trees and pollination by bees everywhere.

I am from hot summers, cool winters and trips to the mountains.

I am from beaches and sunshine with foggy winter fountains.

I am from being the interior designer with a decorating heart.

I am from lessons in spirituality and turning away from the dark.

I am from new motherhood, the best baby and
long afternoon naps.

I am from hoping and dreaming with faith all thrown in.

I am from subdivisions, new homes and California livin'.

I am from earthquakes with mudslides, coastlines plus deserts too.

I am from playgroups and Mum's day out at the Pasadena Zoo.

I am from, Where shall we go next? Will it be Italy? Korea?
Turns out, it's Japan!

I am from Yokohama, the Intelligent Smiling House
and Honmoku dori.

I am from stacking and packing with movers thrown in.

I am from shipments go here, feeling chaos and fear.

I am from what's possible; let's go on an adventure today.

I am from giddyup, let's go; we are now on our way!

Preface

AFTER LIVING IN THE KINGDOM of Saudi Arabia for fifteen years as a corporate spouse, I realized that my journey had changed me in ways unique and profound. I wanted to articulate the adventure we had taken and place a bow on the package, or gift, as it were; thus, the idea for this book was born. Along the way I discovered that friends and colleagues had learned both similar and different lessons. We all agreed, however, on the magic, the mystery and the change we had experienced along the way, together with life lessons including but not limited to gratitude, hospitality and graciousness.

As I turned to life coaching as a profession, I became aware that I was constantly referring to lessons I had learned inside the Arabian adventure. While I witnessed others applying leadership lessons and coaching principles to transform their circumstances, it led me to reflect on how all of us can benefit by sharing each other's stories and lessons. Arabia played a unique role in our multicultural meanderings. While our journey in Arabia was unique and colorful, it was also a high school for life's lessons. I am keen to share the experience in a way that connects us all universally, because I have come to understand that each of us has a precious and unique story that, when articulated, demonstrates the ties of humanity that bind us.

Aramco still claims the title of the largest oil company in the world. As I reached out to men and women who had either worked for Aramco or accompanied a spouse employed by Aramco, I discovered a treasure trove of memories sprinkled across eight decades of experience. It took me years to distill down the conversations and interviews into a coherent manuscript, and before my eyes my own life continued to be transformed by the connection, collegiality and comprehension of these amazing adventurers. The stories that follow share differing perspectives, but one thing we can agree on is that we had an opportunity to live life on a different page from most folk, and we are deeply grateful for the journey and the possibilities that arise when you partner with adventure and trust the process.

Introduction

FREQUENTLY I MEET PEOPLE WHO ask the same questions: "What took you to Arabia?" or "How did you get to Arabia?" I am often flippant and say something like, "By airplane." Neither simple nor flippant answers will ever satisfy the question, nor deliver anywhere near the truth. The vast experiences and challenges that I embraced gave me a connection to humanity I will be forever grateful for. The bottom line is that, like many, we longed for adventure, exploration and a more meaningful life journey; the Camel Lane truly delivered in abundance.

The truth is, most of us love to travel, but why would you transplant your entire life instead of just taking a vacation? What does long-term cultural immersion deliver that settling in one geographical place does not? Living cross-culturally, surrounding ourselves with a different language, food, political system, environment, holidays, celebrations, education and music ultimately transforms your understanding of life and your role on the planet.

Perhaps there should be stickers applied to boarding passes when expats first board their flight to move overseas. One sticker could read "Beware—Expat Living Equals Personal Transformation." A recent survey of expatriates worldwide by Expat Insider 2019 discovered that for U.S. expats alone, over two in five say that they would prefer to live abroad forever. That is striking in itself. Eventually, whether we are interested in armchair travel or have family members or colleagues who have lived overseas, the chances are that each of us is connected in some way, somehow, to someone who has been changed at depth by adventuring overseas.

Millions of people across the globe are actively and thoughtfully choosing long-term expatriation or even immigration as a tool for adventure, a career path or simply a method to express their authentic soul-self. The choice frequently requires making big decisions then living out the consequences of those choices.

The world is more commercially interconnected than ever before. Yet, individuals and nations express fragmentation and isolation. People are ultimately members of symbiotic tribes dependent on each other to solve world problems, maintain peace and live harmoniously. The question is, who do we have to become in order to fill this mandate? And how will we achieve this? Life in the Camel Lane seeks to share our journey of becoming global citizens with some of the peaks, valleys and bewildered coddiwompling that occur along the way.

There are as many ways to describe living in The Kingdom of Saudi Arabia as there are people who go there. The Kingdom of Saudi Arabia can be called Saudi or Arabia, KSA or Saudi Arabia, or after a period residing there, simply, the Magic Kingdom.

Every adventure ultimately has its own unique anatomy and is a container of time, energy and experiences. Arrivals, adaptation and acclimatization are critical when we physically change geographical locations. In modern-day society we have access to such high-speed transportation methods that we often overlook the necessary steps for bringing ourselves fully present and into a mindful relationship with a new place and entirely new people. Adaptation frequently demands sacrifice, steely-eyed focus and tenacity. Enculturation can be a long, slow process of falling in love with a new reality.

Liminal living is the practice of being constantly in-between two cultures and juggling them both. This journey requires that we take action, move out of our comfort zone and cross thresholds, leaving behind old ideas and ways of living. Human nature carries us forward through the journey of transformation whether we cooperate or resist. Living liminally is often uncomfortable and disorienting; nevertheless, Western women in Saudi were frequently required to do so for not only years but sometimes decades. New pastimes, support systems, skills and situations led us ultimately to a new way of being. We learned to juggle cultures, time zones, languages, mindsets, political systems—all the while allowing these influences to inform a new wisdom and understanding about how life works.

Ultimately our paradigms change. We see things differently after living in a cross-cultural experience; we start to view circumstances through a different lens. Our paradigms provide a philosophical framework and for some of us our views change drastically as a result of living not only within the structure of the Saudi society but also within the corporate culture of Saudi Aramco. After 9/11, the ensuing Iraq war and a few years of terrorism in the Kingdom, we had the option to change our minds or our paradigms or to depart. After living in Arabia through these times, we were in some manner different at our core.

Eventually we manage the messiness and disruption and ultimately arrive at a new comfort zone, where we reconcile ourselves to a different way of being and find comfort in an entirely new version of life, one we had never conceived of. By embracing and falling in love with this new iteration, we have the opportunity to expand and share our appreciation of other people and their ways of being.

Ultimately, we pack up our memories, belongings and new experiences and move on. Nevertheless, we grieve. Our losses have a role to play in defining our new identities and sense of belonging. Our grief can define us, or it can serve to ignite and refuel us for new adventures. We can grieve the loss of friends who became family, the physicality of living in a desert and all the wonderful experiences it served up to us, not to mention a lifestyle, colleagues, pastimes and pets left behind.

Re-entry and repatriation require we shift gears and eventually move home to commence a new life. After learning to communicate with other cultures, to live with grit and grace, constantly practicing tolerance and compassion, it can be challenging to resume a life back home. When we pack up for the homecoming, we also pack up new behaviors and hidden skills. We carry them onward either back home or onto the next assignment. Our newly gained perceptions and experiences serve to build the foundation for our next adventure.

The world is full of both wanderers and settlers; both are necessary for balance. If you are a wanderer or a wannabe adventurer, I hope this work gives you the impetus to live outside your previous mental, emotional and physical borders, to explore and enjoy the wonder of this planet's people and cultures. If you are a settler and an armchair traveler, I hope this work provides an insight into how global influence and culture can serve to connect you to the rest of the world.

The way we choose to respond to a life of global mobility has the power to transform each of us into a new person.

The life cycle of an expatriate constantly revolves around the idea of home, identity and belonging. Though we start as one shape, as our global heart grows, our internal geometry changes. Who knows what you might transform into?

Whoever you are and wherever you reside, may your global heart be stretched to include Saudi Arabia, the Middle East and the good that resides within its wonderful people.

في يوم من الأيام

Part 1
WAKING UP!

All journeys have secret destinations of which
the traveler is unaware

Martin Buber

Chapter 1

EXPAT LIFE—A CALL TO ADVENTURE

THREE THINGS STAND OUT ABOUT that interview in Houston. First, it was April Fools' Day; second, the babe in my arms was exactly twenty-one days old; finally, it all seemed so easy and natural. We were visiting the corporate headquarters of the largest oil company in the world, where our tiny family was being interviewed for a position with Aramco, yes, the entire family, colicky babe and all. This event implied that we would, at some point, live in Saudi Arabia.

The Middle East had always held a sense of welcome and hospitality for me. Having lived in Dubai as a single woman working for an oil field contractor from 1976 to 1980, I thought I had a clue! It turns out, I had only a vague sense of the possibilities and the cultures, both corporate and Arabic. Little did I know that both the American corporate culture and the Saudi Arabian cultures had built into them a world of difference from my last experience in Dubai. I was eager to dive in, thrilled at the prospect of a reprise, a do-over or an update of my previous adventure.

While my husband and I had both enjoyed overseas assignments individually, this was to be our first international adventure together. As a recent resident and green-card holder in the US, I was, of course, already overseas. Little did I realize how much I would grow, discover and process during what could be called a humdinger of a journey. Prior to departing the US, I jokingly told people how much I had loved living in Dubai in the 1970s, but I apparently hadn't learned all the lessons I needed to learn while there. Note to self: never joke with the Universe! In my mind the trip was already framed as a deliberate and in some ways political act, intended to support each of our family of three in growing up. Little did I comprehend the personal growth and transformation each of us would enjoy.

An overseas assignment is neither a tourist's nor a traveler's experience. If a tourist's experience is like taking a shower, and a long-term traveler's experience is akin to taking a bath, then the settled expat's is being thrown into the deep end of a swimming pool. Immersion opens the doors for environment, foreign mindset and culture to make deep, unconscious change within us. Juggling new languages, foods and people offers an unparalleled opportunity to master adaptability in all quadrants of living. Prior to every expat assignment, I read voraciously, studied geographical and cultural details of the place and spent time imagining or daydreaming about what it would be like. This always eased the process of arrival, but reality never, ever matched my mental picture. Each destination had been so much bigger and better when my senses finally had the opportunity to wrap themselves around the physical environment and I could soak up the experience. My first ninety days in Arabia were more awkward than graceful.

As our squawking baby was being cared for by an HR person downstairs, the formal interview turned more into a chat over a cup of coffee including catching up on Aramco's changes and growth since I had left the Gulf in 1980. Aramco had been the largest client for the oil field contractor I had worked for at the time, and we found ourselves exchanging gossip about people I had known.

In the end, our Arabian adventure spanned almost two decades. Our personal motivation at the start was a combination of fleeing a predictable life, an economic emergency and the magnetism of adventure. Yes, we lived in California, had a lovely community of people we enjoyed and thrived among. Yes, we had a shiny, brand-new home and a new baby—we were already reveling in new beginnings on every level. On the other hand, we had hopes, dreams and visions for an undetermined but even better reality for all of us. In other words, we were more keenly interested in adventure than predictability.

DISCONTENT AND LONGING

Throughout my life, discontent has been like the parrot sitting on my shoulder, chattering in my ear. I have enjoyed no shortage of longings. Consistently, the possibility of something or somewhere more fun, fascinating or fulfilling has pulled me forward. These impulsions led to assignments with the Foreign & Commonwealth Office in London then Cameroon and later corporate America while in Dubai in my late twenties. In hindsight I recognize these opportunities were a pipeline for me to discover more learning and personal growth. It seems that the best adventures leave one with the sense of having fallen down a rabbit hole, head over heels in love with life, with very little preparation, training or awareness. I was ill-prepared, emotionally challenged and in over my head–perhaps these are all requirements that differentiate an adventure from a settled lifestyle.

Prior to signing with Aramco, John and I were quite frankly at several crossroads. My first child was born in my late thirties, my growing interior design business was flourishing and profitable, yet John needed to make a career change. His contracting job was complete, and he was seeking the next big idea.

John's mother was British, a World War II bride born in Dublin, who married an American pilot. They raised several Third Culture Kids (TCKs—children growing up outside of their parents' native cultures). Several of his formative years were spent in Japan and a portion of his military career in Europe. He was already subconsciously primed for an international lifestyle. When the Aramco opportunity arose, I was willing to relinquish my business, take off on another foreign adventure and never look back.

Our interview was so natural and easy-going it seemed like, yes, this was the easiest decision in the world to say yes to. Although John was the employee being interviewed, the company was very well aware that a supportive and adventuresome spouse was a critical part of the package. Again and again this was reiterated in the interview, how did I feel about the Middle East? Would I be comfortable living in Arabia, given my experience of Dubai? Of course, Dubai was always light-years ahead of Saudi in that era, in terms of choice and freedom. Every answer within me was a yes.

While we were being pulled by adventure, simultaneously we were feeling pushed by some pretty uncomfortable personal circumstances. We were ripe for a big change. The timing was perfect, opportunity beckoned, and we ran—we did not walk—toward it. We followed the yes!

Little did we know when we set out how the journey would unfold and how we would be eternally changed. We knew when we said yes to the job, we'd eventually end up in Arabia, but we didn't know when or how many stops there'd be before we got there. Our next twenty years would take us to Los Angeles, Yokohama in Japan, Ras Tanura then Dhahran in Saudi Arabia and finally Houston, Texas. I wonder in hindsight, did I spend a large part of my life wandering like a camel? We returned in 2010 to the US, I as a retiree from Aramco, a middle-aged woman with adventure under my belt and a brand-new college entrant. At the time we left, we were so captivated by the possibilities of traveling overseas and building a new life that unraveling our old lives seemed a small price to pay.

Later on, during the re-entry phase, which is rarely if ever mentioned prior to departure, we were to discover that reconnection, reorientation and redesigning our lives once more would require focus and attention beyond what we ever imagined.

MOVE BY BABY STEPS

Our opening act of our grand adventure consisted of a two-and-a-half-year journey to even reach the sandy shores of Ras Tanura. That journey was not without its challenges. I temporarily became a single parent when Lynsey was nine months old—remaining behind in Bakersfield, California, our first assignment, for about nine months while John commuted to Pasadena, where the initial refinery project engineering assignment would commence, and returned home on weekends.

Eventually, we all moved south to San Gabriel, adjacent to the city of Pasadena. We were thrilled to be together as a family without the two-hour commute to Bakersfield every weekend. The following year was filled with drama. Massive wildfires burned the hillsides in Altadena. Homes were razed to the ground and hundreds of others were damaged. We watched for days as the hills raged with fire and plumes of angry smoke crowned our new neighborhood. After the fires, mudslides precipitated by earlier fires in the Malibu area caused more damage, and the final trifecta of our Southern California experience was the Northridge earthquake in January of 1994. When the earthquake hit, John bounded out of bed and flew into Lynsey's nursery, exactly the opposite of the recommended behavior. Even this earthquake taught us lessons we would require in Japan a few months later.

It took us much longer to be assigned to a position in Arabia compared to most of our colleagues, who departed from an orientation in Houston straight to Dhahran. I call those the "bonus years." Japan was a delicious and spectacular adventure and an enormous endeavor of learning the language and navigating the metropolis of Yokohama. That period was filled with joy that continues to resonate in the form of memories, friendships and physical decorations we surround ourselves with even today. Wherever I go in our house, memories of Japan envelop us, from a tansu chest displaying sculptured ikebana containers to wedding kimonos that line our entry walls and omamori pouches collected at the temples. Not only do experiences stick to our souls, but stuff also sticks to our bags; we returned with both visible and invisible treasures.

DRAMATIC TRANSITIONS

Leaping into adventure requires making changes, often without the benefits of incremental steps or gradual stages. Fast decision-making is a skill that builds; small decisions made frequently lead to confidence in making larger choices. The decision to say yes and move from Bakersfield was small; *It will only be a few months,* we thought, then the next move to Japan was larger. But "It's only for a few months or a year," we heard ourselves say. Until finally we made the ultimate trip into the Kingdom of Saudi Arabia (KSA) with the intention to stay permanently, with no contract end date in sight. It seemed each move was a step that led naturally to the following one, and each of them was like a step on a staircase. Our perspectives changed as we progressed along the journey.

Overseas adventures frequently require placing life possessions in storage and, for many, not touching these belongings sometimes for several decades. Emotional farewells to friends and family are never easy. I can still vividly remember walking to the white van with the name of my business, Transdesigns Custom Decorating, scrolled along the outside, fastening our seat belts and driving away, headed south from Bakersfield to Pasadena. Inside I was a mixture of emotions and excitement—feeling like I had just stepped off a precipice and was flying through the air unsupported. While my physical senses were enjoying business as usual in the form of an ordinary seatbelt, a windscreen and a boring freeway in front of me, I was driving away from my professional design business.

I remember most of those seminal farewells as if they were seared into my brain. Leaving behind a life I had loved in Bakersfield, a business I had coaxed into life from one single idea, along with a tightknit community was like jumping out of a plane not knowing where you might land. Yet, apparently we humans are much more adaptable and flexible than we think. I believe that packing up your life, moving halfway around the world, establishing a new routine and rhythm, creating new beliefs and growing a global mindset are the best transformational journeys a person can live.

We had packed several shipments: one to take to Japan, another that was to be stored short-term in the US to eventually go to Saudi and a third, which would remain in the US until our final return. I noticed that the curation, packing and maintenance of paraphernalia and furnishings required an inordinate amount of energy.

A critical step in the journey is creating and communicating an articulate vision with everyone involved, and it needs to be visceral and clear in order to carry you through the experience. Much of the process may seem messy, confusing and overwhelming, but order will eventually emerge out of the chaos if you stick to your vision. Our vision was merely a broad outline of a better life, lacking in specifics and pictures. I believe had we fine-tuned it, written more details down, our transitions may have required less energy. Finally, baby steps will take you everywhere—all around the globe in fact. Being willing to take the quantum leap means being satisfied with small steps first.

Our leap happened in steps from Bakersfield to Pasadena, from Pasadena to Yokohama and finally on December 1, 1995, we took that short hop from Bahrain to finally land in Dammam International Airport.

It would be March 1996, almost twenty-four long months since we packed that shipment, before we laid eyes on it again. It would be 2010, about seventeen years later, before we unpacked our long-term shipment and belongings. The reality of what short-term and long-term really mean was a lesson in itself!

Chapter 2

ARRIVALS—GRACEFUL OR GAWKY

ARRIVING WELL IS A SKILL that we are rarely taught. Arrivals steep us in novelty, fascination and sometimes challenging environments. Usually we are so enthralled and in the present that we just allow our senses to absorb reality as it unfolds around us. Many of my friends and colleagues who arrived in Arabia could recount their arrival in incredibly specific detail.

On my own arrival, as I exited the airplane door, took a deep breath and walked down the steps to once again touch terra firma, I looked around and drank in the exotic atmosphere of Bahrain, a short 12-hour layover on the way into Arabia. Those first few moments in the Middle East remain imprinted on my memory. I remember gazing up to the dark, starry sky and being struck by the position of the moon, which seemed to be lying on its side—not quite upright and feeling that it was not where it normally rests in the Western Hemisphere. It felt like a premonition, simultaneously disturbing and peaceful, of some sort of internal shift to come. When my feet hit the tarmac, I was walking into a fresh, wide-open future.

I remained in this strange and wonderful part of the world for the next fifteen years. If at that moment you had told me that this long sojourn was how the trip would unfold, I would have said you were crazy. During those two decades with Aramco, the internet was launched, the world became more interconnected, and the United States invaded then departed Iraq. Our story seemed to parallel that of a shrinking globe: massive diversity and greater opportunities for intercultural understanding and faith surrounded us. Walking down those steps with John, I trusted that the giant leap we had just made was going to be an expansive experience full of opportunity and possibility. I couldn't have known to what extent relocating would shift my perspective on just about everything. There was no sign that said, "Welcome to the Middle East. Prepare yourself for a life-changing experience."

"WHERE AM I?"

This Middle Eastern adventure living and working in KSA was certainly not unique to me. Expatriates since the early 1930s have made thousands of similar trips to this same part of the world. Eight decades of history have happened since the inception of Aramco. Many employees have, in fact, spent entire lifetimes, sometimes spawning several generations of families and launching their progeny as world citizens from the Kingdom of Saudi Arabia. While those steps from an airliner to the tarmac were small, for me the entire experience was a quantum leap. Nowadays, quantum leap ideas are bandied around as if they are commonplace. The notion that humans can make great strides of faith, taking enormous jumps in consciousness and changing their reality through their thinking is run-of-the-mill. I do know that none of these ideas were top of my mind as I slowly navigated those stairs with our three-year-old daughter.

Early the following morning, we enjoyed a long walk on the old Bahrain Corniche. We saw some old piers and dhows lying on their sides in the shallow waters. These graceful, hand-built fishing and sailing vessels are to this day commonly used in the Middle East to transport fish and other goods locally. Today, if we were to take that same walk, it would be on the side of a four-lane highway at the base of two fifty-three-story twin towers. This area is now Bahrain's most prestigious address and a premier commercial development on the seashore. Synchronized, colored lighting in these two towers flows from floor to floor in the evenings and can be seen from miles away, signaling that this land is a twenty-first-century beacon for progress and success. Our stay back then was an overnight layover prior to flying from Bahrain to Dhahran in Saudi Arabia, a distance of only about fifty miles.

The following morning, we landed in an old, shabby, disorganized, low-ceilinged terminal with lines of expatriates from Europe, Pakistan, Bangladesh, the Philippines, Sri Lanka, India and Indonesia. Multiple flights arrive simultaneously, thus depositing thousands of migrant workers into the Kingdom. Untidy lines, a cacophony of languages, much gesticulating and women covered in shapeless black robes stand out vividly in my recollection.

Each person's papers had to be inspected and their visas checked. Eventually an Aramco representative met and whisked us into the Kingdom with relative expediency (at least for that part of the world). A colleague drove us up to Ras Tanura, a distant settlement and compound situated on the periphery of a huge refinery on the shores of the Arabian Gulf.

The ride to our new village compound and our company house from the airport was just fifty minutes. The small compound we were assigned to was a soporific little beach community on the Strait of Hormuz just across from Iran. With my face pressed up against the window, the journey from Dhahran to Ras Tanura unfolded in a landscape devoid of color, detail and obvious life. I was hoping for a camel sighting or even a Bedouin tent but was met with power lines, a gray desert, overcast skies and bleakness. Driving onto the compound for the first time and navigating the security gates, it dawned on me that we were entering a different world, even more rare than the Arabian reality. The compound was organized Western-style with wide streets, cul-de-sacs and front lawns. Homes with red-tiled Western roofs were arranged in predictable patterns, just like in the US. It all seemed somehow shabby and slightly rundown after Japan. However, we were determined to be optimistic, and when we saw the location of our new home, right on the corner of Sand Dollar and Surfboard streets, that lifted our spirits. We were a three-minute walk to a beach—oh joy, this seemed like an omen.

On our first morning in Ras Tanura, we took our second walk along a seafront, as we had in Bahrain. This one was very different. We awoke early, put on our walking shoes and went out the door looking for the action. There was none. Everyone else was asleep;

we did not see one other soul. After Yokohama, a dynamic, bustling city of 11 million people, this sleepy settlement was a shock to the system. It felt like we had been dropped onto a distant planet—a deserted golf resort planet. For the next eighteen months living in Ras Tanura, golf carts were the preferred mode of transportation.

SHOCK AND SURPRISE

Our arrival in Ras Tanura was marked by a twenty-day spell of rain, almost unheard of in the KSA. *How coincidental*, I thought, as I felt a bit like an anomaly myself. I remember peering out of our house window at the street, seeing drains unable to cope with red sandy water flowing like a tumbling river. In the days to come, I would stare out that same window looking for people. There was little activity, except for the morning and evening commute to work and school. I struggled to make sense of this foreign environment, the culture and its people. It was like living behind a curtain. My sense of isolation was made even more pronounced by our distance from the outside world. We arrived on December 1, 1995, just three years post-Gulf War. Prior to the Gulf War, there was little possibility of exiting and returning to the Kingdom at will due to visa restrictions; you essentially lived "in Kingdom" full time and passports were held at the passport office. For scheduled departures and visits home, employees had to apply to gain access to their passports, then go through some bureaucracy prior to physically leaving the Kingdom.

After the Gulf War, many restrictions were lifted, and everyone took great pains to explain to us how much more freedom we should be grateful for. I certainly didn't get that sense in the first ninety days.

One of our "freedoms" was apparently the ability to watch television. Although we were told that TV satellites were banned, we were surprised to see them scattered around our compound, and they were even in Arabic compounds "on the economy," and attached to desert settlements.

ISOLATION

We had very limited television, mostly the Aramco Channel. By January when Ramadan arrived, I remember being hypnotized watching thousands of pilgrims on TV circumambulating the Kabaa, also known as the Great Mosque of Mecca. The American Forces Network (AFN) is the broadcast service operated by the United States American Forces Radio and Television Service. The service was no longer available after the Gulf War, which affected Ras Tanura so acutely, yet everyone talked about it as if it were still on the air. We had TV and I concluded that we were fortunate to get even those few hours a day of pilgrims. The contrast between the liveliness and upbeat energy of Yokohama, which we had just left behind, and the colorless, quiet lifestyle of the desert was striking.

Slowly, slowly technology crept in and within the next eighteen months to three years we were blessed with internet access (albeit the slow dial-up version), and other technological advances such as the international phone service Vonage. Ultimately a video calling service shrank our world and gave us a solid connection to friends and family in the UK and US. This progression took about three years. With no internet at first, no Snapchat, Facebook or even email, I felt very isolated from my previously vibrant life.

Arrivals imply that everything is happening for the first time. We heard the call to prayer within hours of arriving and would hear another 25,000 plus over our sojourn. Arrivals demand that we learn how to navigate the culture, learn the rules, such as how to call a taxi, where to collect the mail, how to address an Arab man, how to subtly acknowledge an Arab woman covered head to toe in black, how to pass through the security gates, know where I could and could not drive. In hindsight, I would assign myself about a six out of ten on my arrival, if I were being graded.

Within a few weeks, we started adjusting to the slower pace of the compound. My daughter attended preschool, and I had time on my hands to explore. As I began to venture out, I quickly learned many things about the local culture and customs. Prior to arriving in KSA, for example, all expatriates were required to pledge to be good guests and to honor the local customs—everything from not drinking alcohol to women keeping covered and fully clothed while in public. I distinctly remember walking to the gym wearing what I considered to be relatively tasteful exercise gear that I assumed would mollify the local Saudi population; but when a Saudi security guard followed me for five blocks in his car, I wasn't sure whether to laugh or be dismayed. Perhaps it was because I was a new face in this small community, or did he feel that I needed protection?

The background of our life in Saudi became like the signature tune of our living movie: this was the call to prayer. The call to prayer occurred five times every day without fail, moving a few minutes each day as the sunrise and sunset times changed. Our cycles were closely tied to the natural movements of the planet. Vacations and holidays were determined by the Hijri calendar, which coordinated with the daily rising and setting of the sun. All the Muslim holidays including Ramadan and Eid, are planned around the Hijri calendar. Expatriate families in the Aramco compound were, for the most part, permitted to practice their faith privately, but in the cities and other expatriate compounds, this was most keenly discouraged and was considered a punishable offense. The import of Bibles, crosses and Christmas trees was prohibited, and yet, magically, the ubiquitous "Holiday Trees" (as Christmas trees are known) were found throughout the compound, and rarely a couple were brought in for sale in the Commissary on camp. Many of us somehow managed to sneak in one tree via a shipment or in the back of a car across the causeway from Bahrain.

Arriving in December as we did, we anticipated a few Christmas festivities on the compound but were surprised by the number of parties and amount of caroling. And people dressed up as Santa Claus were everywhere! In fact, we had to be vigilant to keep Lynsey from the front window, where Santas went whizzing by in golf carts. In retrospect, that first holiday in Ras Tanura was a pivotal time during which we adjusted from the Zen culture of Yokohama—with its activity, traffic, densely populated high-rise buildings, modern architecture and international diversity—to the quiet, calm, modulated energy on a somewhat isolated compound.

BUILDING COMMUNITY

We lived surrounded by gates, fences, security guards and (after 9/11) layers of sophisticated technology. While this was intended for our safety and security, what I didn't expect was how quickly it became normal and how being locked in together somehow engendered trust, respect and esteem between the expatriate and Arabic communities. Although the bonds of tribes and families run deep, the alliances formed in our expat community were as potent and powerful as any tribe. In fact, the expatriate community came to reflect many small tribes, divided into groups according to interests. There were dozens of activities and creative pursuits to dive into. Dozens of nationalities were represented in the company, and this provided all of us with the opportunity to enjoy intimate cultural diversity.

I eventually began to learn to respect and trust the Arabs' abiding sense of destiny and well-being, which embraced health, happiness and prosperity. That vague feeling seemed to permeate the souls of many of the Arabs I befriended. For the most part, when Saudi women unveiled to reveal their faces, what I observed were warm, glowing eyes that gave me a peaceful reassurance there was a person, or an energetic presence that was almost larger than life, under the cloth. *Is it possible that being cloaked for so many decades, these women have had the time and space to build their own powerful sense of being from within?* I wondered. I was privileged to meet many well-educated Saudis, part of the privileged strata of society, who spoke English well. Many of us came to understand and empathize with the amazingly rapid history of change and modernization that has overtaken these desert dwellers.

Although my arrival felt disjointed and unsteady, in many ways that was the result of changing frequencies or energy levels and habits we had adopted in Japan. Every arrival requires a few hours, days or months for us to naturally join the rhythm or flow of the place we are arriving in.

Chapter 3

WESTERN WOMEN MEET MIDDLE EASTERN MINDSET

NOT EVERYONE IS ROPED INTO the expat life with enthusiasm and delight. Many corporate wives came unwillingly but bravely to show good faith. Personal leadership lessons were constantly on offer through both the corporate and native cultures. I saw Western women arriving like mice who transformed into lions, advocating for their families, themselves and their passions like gladiators in the Colosseum.

When Jenny's husband, Omar, brought up the idea of moving to Arabia, Jenny was not only angry, but according to her, she was "belligerent and really awful." She kept asking me, "What do you expect me to do? This was primarily about Omar and his career." He was working seventy to eighty hours per week as a journalist, with a limited salary, and the opportunity to move to Arabia to work for

Aramco and cross that professional bridge to public relations was the most marvelous dream he could imagine.

He found the corporate brochures, paperwork and application forms on top of the garbage where Jenny had placed them. She did eventually bring them back into the house, where she and Omar struck a deal to make it work for three to five years. She had veto rights and could at any point declare her option to leave, at which point they would give themselves a year to gather everything together and move on. Jenny did eventually exercise those veto rights while on vacation in 2006. Everyone had differing tolerances for the lifestyle and possibilities.

TRAILER LIVING

In 1975, a somewhat tentative twenty-six-year-old Vicci arrived with her husband and two young children in Abqaiq, a smaller compound known as "the friendly city," thirty-eight miles west of Dhahran. Company housing was provided by contractors who reported to Aramco. They lived with thirty to forty other families in triple-wide trailers.

Vicci's dad had retired from the Army Corps of Engineers when she was a child, and the family had bought a travel trailer and journeyed extensively to Canada, Mexico and seemingly everywhere in between. Vicci viewed this lifestyle as a contributing factor to her desire for adventure and travel. Her mum used to say, "We have gypsy feet." When Vicci set off on her adventures in Arabia and beyond, she blithely took her two children everywhere. Frequently it was neither easy nor pleasant; however, the children became the very best of travelers, never complaining nor asking, "Are we there yet?" They were prepared for long, arduous and tedious journeys and mastered travel early on.

With one family per trailer, living in tight proximity to each other, a real sense of community was built quickly. Vicci says, "They were fairly gross, with a rust carpet, white Naugahyde furniture and full faux walnut paneling throughout. They had a washer but no dryer, so everything had to be dried outside." Now, Arabia is a country that endures some of the greatest *shamals*, huge sand- and windstorms, on the planet. This circumstance was never conducive to clean laundry. January 1975 was also one of the wettest years in Arabian history. Downpours galore with water seemingly everywhere. The trailer leaked. Pots, pans and every container possible were lined up along the seams to catch those leaks. Because the trailers were contractor-owned, Aramco was of little assistance.

There were no telephones in the trailers; everyone shared a phone attached to a pillar outside. In order to call the contractor to come and repair the leaks, one had to stand outside in the rain to make the call. Vicci's family lived there for several months before being assigned a family home. If you had one or two children the same sex, you were assigned a two-bedroom home. With two children who were different genders, you were assigned a three-bedroom house. Telephone calls on the shared line had to be booked well in advance and were several dollars per minute. Calling home was a rare luxury and not available at the drop of a hat.

Change occurred all the time and depending on the era you arrived in Arabia, together with the assignment you had come to work on, your circumstances could be vastly different. Many families lived in large compounds surrounded by other expats with opportunities for every sport under the sun. Others arrived into tiny distant communities on far-flung pipeline jobs, or were simply contract employees in the industry and could find themselves living in the heart of the Saudi culture isolated from anyone or anything remotely familiar. It took all sorts of grit and guts to handle many of the conditions.

BIG ADVENTURE INSIDE THE TRUE ARABIA

Jacque graduated from college in 1985, immediately married her Greek boyfriend and within two weeks was living in the desert town of Hofuf in the Eastern Province of Saudi Arabia. Jacque's husband was hired by a Greek friend, who was the general engineer for a local construction company. The company's name was Basma, which means "happy." Jacque felt completely isolated, a cultural misfit living alongside Saudis. She credits this period as the single most pivotal experience in growing up. She said, "It made me a much stronger and well-rounded person."

Hofuf was extremely remote, even for Saudi Arabia. It was a medium-size desert town close by the Al-Hasa Oasis and had one main street and a *souk* (a market that sells one single type of product). The oasis is one of the largest in Saudi and is twenty-five miles west of the Persian Gulf. Imagine 30,000 acres, a bit larger than the city of Paris, packed full of palm trees and other crops fed by artesian underground springs.

Jacque lived what we called "out on the economy." There were no protective compounds for foreigners in Hofuf. Living on the economy meant that she had to shop in local stores and participate in local Arabian life. Home was a tiny apartment above a Saudi family and across the street from the local mosque on a dirt road. She had no Western neighbors. She stood out in the community as "The Westerner." Being the only blonde in town, she was like a lamppost on a deeply dark night. There was only one small supermarket in town; most weekends were spent driving 90 miles each way across the desert to Al Khobar and the Aramco compound to hunt down groceries. Scoring a box of mac and cheese to bring home for dinner during the week was a cause for exultation and great glee.

Eventually, one Austrian woman moved a few miles away. There were no taxis back then; locals in these small towns walked everywhere to visit family and neighbors, and the local men owned small Toyota trucks. On rare occasions, either Jacque or her friend's husband would drop them off at each other's home. They discovered a common pastime: knitting. The Austrian lady brought high-quality yarn from Austria and they would knit together. To this day Jacque is an accomplished knitter and artist who exhibits regularly.

Without the benefit of TV, internet and zero social life in Hofuf, Jacque's days were spent knitting, exercising using old cassette tapes smuggled into the country and reading books—a solitary existence. She and her husband planned their social life for the weekends when they would drive up to the big city of Dhahran to visit friends on the Aramco compound, shop in Al Khobar and enjoy a Friday brunch at the International Hotel. Jacque was shocked to discover what she had gotten herself into.

The Kingdom of Saudi Arabia has become a modern economy only in the last few decades. There are some practices that most Westerners consider barbaric. Shariah law required that punishment be dished out in public. Public gatherings for this purpose have become rare, but back in the 1980s public punishments were common.

Jacque and her husband were politely and warmly invited to stay around and witness stonings, lashings or even beheadings on Fridays after Mosque in Hofuf. On Thursday afternoons, locals would line up several small white Toyota pickup trucks piled high with stones. Occasionally a woman would be punished for perceived infidelities. As the stoning wall was right by their house, they had to contend with this weekly event. At every opportunity they left town in order to avoid facing such macabre behavior. Jacque witnessed so many shocking sights that she takes very little for granted nowadays. On the one hand the Saudi people were consistently nice to her. Personally, one to one, they were welcoming, friendly and smiling. On the other hand, their Shariah laws, beheadings, wearing the *abaya* and tribal behavior seemed brutal. Jacque's adventure was dramatic and three decades later still informs her life choices.

LIFESTYLE AND HEALING

Julie came to Arabia unsettled, stressed out and looking for something vastly different. For the four-and-a-half years prior, she had been employed by Shell at the Deer Park manufacturing complex in Texas, the sixth-largest chemical complex in the world at that time, as an industrial hygienist in the health, safety and environmental field. Her team dealt with railway collisions, damages or leaks related to Shell chemical products.

Julie's journey to Arabia required huge changes to shed a professional position and identity and transform into a stay-at-home housewife in Dhahran, before reentering the workforce again. Being captain of an Emergency Response team had required being available in the middle of the night, a cell phone by the bed and even within range while on vacation. Being on-call 24/7 for 365 days per year armed with two pagers, two cell phones and occasionally two mobile radios was grueling, a challenging ride fueled by adrenaline and stress. A nanny accompanied their daughters to school and took care of them after school. Quality family time was extremely rare.

Ultimately, Julie's health was compromised; therefore, her family consciously looked for a healthier adventure. Living and working in a community like Dhahran, which dedicated itself to providing well-being in so many ways and to building successful families, was very inviting.

Initially, Julie was one of the army of stay-at-home mums who lived on the compound. The adjustment from a round-the-clock job to having a houseboy and a gardener and being free in terms of where to spend her time and energy were gifts she welcomed with open arms. After a couple of years she was grateful to go back to work and use her high-level skills, although working as a female surrounded by Saudi men could frequently offer struggle. Many Western women walked a fine line of dealing with Middle Eastern males at work, on the compound and in town. It could be both frustrating and challenging to the our core feminist tendencies.

THE ABAYA—TO WEAR OR NOT?

The customs of the Kingdom of Saudi Arabia have flexed and wended their way across hundreds of years of history and multiple generations of style, and yet women in the Middle East continue to be viewed as if living in the Middle Ages in part due to their choice of public apparel—the abaya. Modesty becomes an immediate issue for Western women arriving in Arabia. I so remember struggling with "what shall I wear?" every time I left the house for the first month or so. In fact, this seems to be the largest issue that Westerners are aware of in relation to the culture of KSA. Returnees are constantly asked, "Did you have to cover?" Like almost everything in Arabia, the answer was never a simple yes or no. Mystique, tradition, history, religion and personal preference all seem to converge around the subject of wearing abayas.

The perspective of women throughout the Middle East around abayas varies tremendously. From Afghanistan and Iran to Saudi Arabia and beyond, traditions, personal preferences and historical precedents defy the grasp of the Western mind. One thing to remember is that Saudi women for the most part enjoy their culture and are willing to happily wear the abaya based on years of tradition and religion, melding it with a modern and contemporary lifestyle. To justify a complete discussion on this subject a number of books would be required, so I will only refer to a few examples that friends and I experienced.

Upon arrival at the Saudi airports it becomes quickly evident that many women cover. Scantily clad western clothing is not the norm; however, if it is camouflaged by a traditional garment–no problem. Arabic women frequently wear abayas and Western women are found in a motley assortment of attire. If one arrives improperly dressed, there are instant signals including shuffling of feet, sideways glances, challenging stares and sometimes outright comments. Often the customs and other officials used to become agitated and push you to the front of the line in order to get you through the airport without creating a scene.

Every non-Arab woman has a different experience with the abaya. Most of the women I knew had experiences on the Aramco bus going into Khobar or while traveling around the Eastern Province when many Arab women would scold us with looks, if not words. Several of the women I interviewed for this book adamantly refused to wear one, while others were happy to capitulate to this local custom. One of my friends who lived there for thirty-plus years never donned an abaya. This was pretty common for women who had arrived in the earlier decades, but many of us who arrived later, particularly post 9/11, arrived into a different system and a different mindset where some were actually grateful for the invisibility cloak an abaya seemed to offer us.

During the fifteen years I spent in Saudi, the garment went through a total evolution, which has continued since my departure. When I arrived in KSA in 1995, you had the choice of buying a (very plain) abaya in a local souk. Dozens of stores in the mall also offered them. Abayas were large shapeless bags made of polyester and, of course, completely black. The fastenings ranged from just a button at the neck to five or six hooks or studs from the neck to below the waist, one at chest level and usually one around the knees—heaven forbid they would blow open and expose a pair of pants, or a muumuu like many of the local women wore or, my goodness, a bare leg. (In the city of Khobar there was a poster often found in expat bathrooms of a Saudi woman striding out with a very long, sexy leg exposed, wearing a garter. These posters are still frequently to be found in returnees' homes.)

By the time I left KSA, there were dozens more stores, and with the advent of technology there are, of course, hundreds of websites offering the garment. I bet if you asked 100 expats who have lived in Saudi, very few women would associate the idea of an abaya with the term "adorable" but there is a brand called Adorable Abayas. Upmarket stores popped up everywhere in almost every mall, outfitted with mirrors, chandeliers and glamorous decorations, selling all kinds of tricked-out abayas. They have become a high-fashion statement, with cuffs, collars, decorative pockets and often colorful sparkles or sequins down the back and along the hem of the garment. The most recent creations are avant-garde and come in fashionable colors.

Prices for abayas can mount into the thousands of dollars, and the options and decorations are varied. The first abaya I purchased was at a small booth in a mall and cost about twenty dollars. In Dhahran there was a wonderful ethnic store called Desert Designs. The owner designed abayas with ethnic fabrics from India, Pakistan and places like Turkmenistan. Abayas came frequently enhanced by ornamentation, including trimming on cuffs, pockets, hems and the opening down the front.

Frequently I attended events where Arab women arrived in abayas looking like visions of elegance. These fashions are driven by the more affluent Arabic women who often have a comprehensive wardrobe of abayas ranging from simple Spartan ones for daytime to diamante-studded ones for evening. My friend Lena would often lend me one of her collection to wear to exotic gatherings.

One could wear as much or as little under the garment as one chose. I personally did not wear the abaya until around 2002, after 9/11 and during the time that terrorist activities rocked KSA.

Initially I hated it. It was uncomfortable, hot, suffocating and frustrating; however, like all new habits, it became second nature. I found that mine was lacking a stud at the bottom. Occasionally on a particularly windy day it would blow open to reveal whatever I was wearing underneath, and I ended up feeling like some whacked-out cartoon character walking down the street while it billowed in the wind behind me ... so much for modesty! I was willing to wear it but was not concerned with the functionality.

Years ago a special dispensation was decreed by the king that Aramco Western wives were exempt from the requirement to wear the abaya. This was not carte blanche to dress scantily. Most women wore pants or skirts and covered their arms while out in public. When expats donned the cloak, it was more a symbol of keeping the peace, respecting local traditions and blending in instead of standing out. Did we still get stared at in the mall? Oh yes—particularly our teenage daughters. Occasionally, I would feel as if we were lightning rods for the attention of young Saudi men when our daughters were with us—no abaya could dissolve their interest in natural, youthful beauty. However, the garment did serve to make us slightly less conspicuous.

THE WOMEN'S MALL

Mary had the joyful experience of an invitation by a Saudi female friend, Foudah, to attend the Women's Mall in Dhahran. This mall sold clothing, goods and materials only to women. Every single person in this mall was a Saudi woman: shopkeepers, shoppers, sales clerks, servers in the coffee shops and even the stock clerks. Had Foudah not instigated this outing, Mary would never ever have known it existed. They went together by taxi and the first thing that struck Mary was the doors of the mall were all tinted glass; no one could see inside.

There was not one single abaya in sight. No one covered their hair. Instead, they were dressed up in high heels or some sort of "house dress," a long, flowing, shapeless garment. The women were brilliantly decked out and in their element. Foudah matter-of-factly requested that Mary remove the headscarf and abaya she was wearing. When Mary asked why, Foudah said, "Just think, if we were allowed to wear our abayas and scarves, don't you think the men out there would disguise themselves, walk in and be perfectly disguised? This way we can all just *be* women."

Mary was fascinated by the display of grit and glamour in a society where women were all but declared invisible. Suddenly, prayer time arrived. The female shopkeepers hustled around closing stores, turning off the lights and ushering customers outside. Instantly these bright, colorful beings morphed like reverse butterflies into their abaya cocoons, transforming back to indistinguishable shapes. Upon exiting the mall they were met by a line of cars, trucks and SUVs with husbands and drivers ready to whisk them off. In the blink of an eye this subculture was swallowed up and shuttled off—almost as if the experience never happened. Mary recalls wondering, *Did that really happen?*

AN INVISIBILITY CLOAK

Upon arriving in Saudi, Michelle faced some professional challenges with a few of the Western personnel at the hospital. The situation was so dire that she retreated into an experiment. Because there was one Commissary on the compound, and the professional single gals worked all day, there was a high chance that shoppers would run into work colleagues or neighbors who were free at the same time. Michelle has dark hair and is a naturally exotic-looking woman, fairly tall with wide-set, dark eyes. One day, she wore an abaya, veil and head scarf and headed for the Commissary. The experience was successful while revealing at the same time. She was able to stand unrecognized inches away from someone she preferred to avoid. This person was completely oblivious and unconcerned by the sight of a fully covered "Arabic" woman in the store.

Michelle enjoyed a feeling of freedom and complete anonymity. Wearing the abaya felt like donning an invisibility cloak, similar to the one in the Harry Potter movies, except the costume was in plain view. You knew there was a person in there, but the feeling the abaya created was of a distinct personal space. The experience left its mark on her.

On another occasion she took the bus to Ras Tanura. Michelle designed this day as a mental health day at the beach, but since she wanted to remain anonymous, she chose to don the disguise to travel.

Upon arriving at Ras Tanura, she walked the short 100 yards to the beach, removed the gear and spent the day relaxing and unwinding. Upon returning in the evening to Dhahran, she was once more Saudi-clothed and was curious about the attention a Lebanese fellow on the bus gave her. He stared at her continuously, repeatedly asking if she spoke English, to which she shook her head and said "la," meaning no. Michelle sensed that he could tell she was not Saudi, although she was fully covered head to foot. *Ah, but what about the feet*, she wondered? Perhaps the flip-flops she was wearing were a clue to her true identity. Saudis are rarely seen wearing flip-flops while covered. Or did he in fact somehow intuit her Western energy emanating from the outfit? Undaunted, this man stared at her all the way to Dhahran, and upon exiting the bus, he gave her a note with his telephone number.

A third attempt at this dress-up experience came when she accompanied her twenty-something daughter to Rashid Mall. The mall is large, full of mirrors, glass, escalators and high-end European designer stores and filled with a population similar to a mini-United Nations. Abaya-clad women glide around as if on wheels. Michelle and Danica decided to go incognito, completely decked out in abayas with *niqabs* to cover their faces, and just observe. Danica had a distinct strut to her walk, and after a few moments they were conscious of drawing stares, attention and general interest. Their attempt to "be" Saudi didn't seem to be fooling anyone. No one paid a bit of attention to Michelle; she paced herself, quieted her energy and seemed to blend in. After a short chat, they decided they needed some strategy. Danica slowed down her gait, took smaller steps, gave up her strut and kept her arms still. Within a short time, they observed they were attracting less attention and diminished curiosity from the locals. After some practice they felt like they could meld into the population and disappear quite effectively.

All these experiences led Michelle to reflect upon the invisibility factor that occurs when wearing an abaya, how it is both an invisibility cloak and an attention-getter depending on how it is worn and who is observing.

I found the abaya conveyed a sense of freedom when visiting

the more traditional city of Dammam. I could roam around, go to the fish market, get in taxis with Saudi drivers, spend time with shopkeepers, bargain with vendors, all with a sense of calmness that would not have been so smooth had I been wearing Western dress. While wearing it I sometimes felt slightly invisible, even with reddish hair uncovered.

I believe that Arab women wear abayas for many reasons, not the least of which is simple tradition. Up until 1980 and around the time of the revolution in Iran, women in Saudi Arabia were wearing loose-fitting muumuu-type garments that still covered the feminine shape, but they were colorful, bright, sometimes even garish. I wonder how many are still around. Recently I met a gal who lived in Arabia in the 1970s. She still rocks the most stylish Bedouin dress, with metal jewelry attached. These garments certainly win the test of time! The colors of her dress are stunningly rich, the garment has style, and the cultural feeling is unmistakable.

Wearing the abaya is an example of how we could change our attitude and behavior and ultimately discover a sense of freedom within an idea we may have resisted for so long. When I first arrived in Saudi, I pledged to never wear one. To me covering seemed to signal negativity, oppression and some sort of undefined unpleasantness. However, in hindsight I am grateful for the opportunity to have worn an abaya and have gotten the briefest glimpse of what life behind it is like.

I doubt that Western women will ever fully understand the Middle Eastern or Muslim women's mindset around the abaya, its uses, traditions and purpose. However, I feel like the opportunity to wear one and to notice how my perspective changed gave me an insight into their lives. Although we don't subscribe to wearing abayas in the West, we do use a similar idea of hiding what we choose not to let others see. The abaya was a cultural tool I am forever grateful to have had the opportunity to play around with. And although I experience an affinity when I see Muslim women wearing a head scarf or an abaya now, I can only guess at their intentions.

Part 2
ADAPTATION

"The real voyage of discovery consists not in seeking new lands but seeing with new eyes."

Marcel Proust

Chapter 4

LEAP FIRST

ARRIVING IN SAUDI IT WAS IMMEDIATELY evident to me that we had arrived on a "man planet." We were greeted by segregated lines in immigration for families and for single males. The officials rarely if ever looked in my eyes. I would discover that this was to become the norm. The idea that women could be treated as if they were totally invisible felt foreign and disconcerting.

Before long we were landed and loaded into that quintessential Saudi carrier, the Chevrolet Suburban. When I got in that Suburban, I had no idea that I was to become a passenger for the next fifteen years of my life, nor did it forecast the willingness I would later demonstrate in being a passenger instead of the driver of my own life. I had no inkling of the challenges, the gifts and the lessons that were part of the package I was beginning to unpack amid this arrival.

SPOILED OR DISILLUSIONED OR BOTH

As promised by the Saudi Aramco website, everything in the community was literally two minutes away. Yes, we had a substantial home, access to small parks within walking distance and the Commissary providing food for the average family. Our house even came with a gardener who adopted us on first sight. He was in his seventies, quite blind, speaking very little English but packing a huge intention to be on our payroll. His efforts with our front yard were rather pathetic, and the small banana tree in the backyard had no chance of ever thriving, yet he persisted, providing water and attention every week.

Yes, there were also two fabulous swimming pools, gyms separate for men and women, a theater, bowling alley and library. The ribbon of sandy beach reaching from Ras Tanura refinery in the north to the no-nonsense compound boundary fencing in the south was compelling and mesmerizing. Yet I felt flawed and insufficient to the task of building a life. It seemed like I was playing a game of hide and seek with ghosts. It all felt somewhat surreal.

I frequently felt a sense of remoteness on the compound, as if on a desert island. It was common to walk around and see not a single soul outside. My senses were craving busy, bustling crowds. I imagined I had space-sickness, a physical sensation astronauts experience. I felt disrupted on all fronts: physically, emotionally and spiritually, like a bobble-toy that could not find upright. I had never arrived anywhere quite like this before.

Just three days prior, I could walk out of my contemporary penthouse perched atop the building known as "The Intelligent and Smiling House" in Yokohama. Emerging outside onto the streets of Japan was a perennial and most curious adventure. Stimulation was everywhere in the form of noisy traffic with incessant sirens, blinking lights on neon signs and endless activity of humanity in motion. I rode a traditional Japanese bicycle to and from the markets with my toddler strapped into the little seat on the back and a basket up front for the precious groceries I had scored that morning. I would frequently purchase unidentifiable food and study the packaging in order to find clues as to how to prepare these offerings. The streets were filled with colorful characters. Little old bent-over ladies perfectly dressed in pressed kimonos, punk rock twenty-year-olds sporting purple and teal hairdos masquerading as the latest personalities from manga comic books, as well as neat ranks of small children walking lockstep, dressed in immaculate yellow school uniforms, were part of my reality.

Fast-forward to Ras Tanura where the natives wore long black or white robes that flickered in the wind. I would see Saudis around the compound, but the sightings were so fleeting that I didn't feel like I was in the midst of a society at all. The "real" Saudi Arabia seemed distant and unreachable in so many ways. Too much time spent on the compound would never help me connect to the essence of this place. A few golf carts and a few cars moved around in the early morning. I was constantly asking, "Where are all the people?" and when I saw them, "Why do they move so slowly?" because my frame of reference was still stuck on Japanese time. It seemed to me that Arabs float while Japanese people bounce.

Perched on the Arabian Gulf, Ras Tanura enjoys a quiet, deeply sheltered beach. The gulf is shallow and enclosed by land on three sides, with a very narrow passage through the Strait of Hormuz into the Gulf of Oman. With few rivers flowing into the Gulf—from Iraq, Iran and Saudi Arabia—it takes between three to three-and-a-half years for the Arabian Gulf to flush its contents. In 1995, we saw vestiges of the Gulf War. When 800 oil wells were blown up at the end of the war, over 600 caught fire and burned while oil gushed into the gulf. Ras Tanura lies just south of Kuwait, which suffered enormous ecological distress. Walking the beach that morning there was still evidence of that holocaust, with small- to medium-size tar balls along the water's edge.

John, being the employee, set off for work the very next morning. He was immediately immersed in the process of getting an ID to enter the refinery where he would be working. Within a couple of days he was ensconced in an office with colleagues, a natural social network and most of all—a purpose. I suddenly realized that my purpose was singular: I was a mum; that was going to have to be enough. The Welcome Lady took me around, showed me the Commissary, the gym, the school, the Golf Shack, the recreation center and so on, and I felt more isolated than ever upon returning "home." I wondered where the community was, and for days I would take walks with Lynsey in the stroller, looking.

THE ART OF GETTING CURIOUS

Heavy-duty canvas, black with cream horizontal stripes, the tent sat on a knoll nestled in a large sand dune. Six or seven irregular, somewhat buckled, knobby wooden posts supported the tent, which seemed to hug the landscape. Sturdy guy ropes pulled it in every direction. Open on one side, the traditional Arabic woven carpets were strewn around to provide comfortable flooring. Low arabesque furniture consisting of long, upholstered benches outlined half the space. The curtain down the middle divided the space between the entertainment or welcoming area for guests and male family members, and the female quarters and domestic accommodations.

Ever since Abraham, considered by many to be the father of the three religions of Islam, Judaism and Christianity, it has been Bedouin tradition to keep at least one side of the tent open. This practice allows the dwellers therein to know when guests, or uninvited strangers, are arriving. In this tent, the opening was rather small; nevertheless, a middle-aged Saudi fellow with a stick and a couple of teenage boys emerged from the tent.

Driving out in the desert a few miles from camp with friends, we were on our way to dig up some sand roses, beautiful clusters of crystal found buried under the sand in the Eastern Province. Adapting to our new lives in Saudi called for not only settling into compound routine but also becoming educated on the traditions, culture and mindset of our hosts, the Saudis. Apparently, there was no better place to learn about Saudi traditions than from the Bedouins themselves, these desert dwellers who for the most part still cling to the ancient culture and practices. In an effort to get educated, off we went.

LEARNING THE LAYERS—DISCERNMENT

The traditional model of cultural adaptation includes the honeymoon followed by culture shock, which leads to recovery and finally adjustment. I felt a bit disoriented and at sea, wondering how I would ever fit into this new reality. Instead of holding the necessary vision of being settled, nestled and comfortable in this strange environment, I was behaving like a hothouse plant in a mad experimental greenhouse. I wasn't focusing on the fun; I found myself preoccupied with how hard it all was. That never goes well and needed to change.

For a while, my adaptation was exhausting. It was not merely a mental exercise but an all-encompassing physical, emotional and spiritual journey. Starting from about week four through week ten or twelve, I went to bed exhausted every night—mostly from trying too hard all day long to like something that I really didn't. In hindsight I learned that while I was in the honeymoon stage of cultural adaptation in some areas, I was already in culture shock in others, and as a seasoned expat who had already lived in the Middle East, I found that I had actually jumped into adjustment in some ways. Two decades prior I had lived in Dubai and spoken Arabic, so hearing and appreciating the language was not difficult; in fact it was welcoming and soothing to me. I had anticipated the social side on the compound to be easy to navigate, but instead I found myself more shocked than inspired.

Not only were we living inside a foreign country, but I found myself hibernating in a bubble inside a bubble, each with differing rules, boundaries, customs and expectations. Naturally the first bubble we found ourselves inside was our company house, which could have been swept up from an American subdivision and dropped on the corner of Surfboard and Sanddollar in the small Ras Tanura compound. Even the structure felt out of place in relation to the earth, with so much comfort and civilization indoors and yet so much desolation, heat and alienation outside.

The next layer of invisible rules and expectations was set by the corporate culture of Aramco. It had not penetrated my mind until I was on the ground that I was actually going to be living inside corporate culture 24/7. All my previous expat assignments I had lived as part of a city. While I understood the purpose and lifestyle of living on a compound, I was not prepared for the adjustment to life in a corporate institution. This alone was later to be worth the price of admission—how many people get the opportunity to view a corporate structure from the inside out round the clock for decades? Aramco truly was an anomaly. The mixture of US and Arabic customs that existed inside the barriers, barbed wire fences, security systems and gates all had to be learned.

Plus, we were never living remotely from Saudi people. A certain amount of interaction and mixing was expected; tolerance and grace were called for straightaway. While we had Saudi neighbors who lived right next door to us, sometimes they felt more distant and inaccessible than the Bedouins living out in the desert. I found it amusing that we felt welcome in some ways and in some places yet not others. The pecking order that existed among expats was the strangest and most alien of all.

I discovered groups of powerful, intelligent, educated and smart women everywhere I turned who were complicit like myself in being relegated to the company nomenclature of "dependent." Initially my instinct was to resist, but I found that resistance was futile and the adaptation needed to happen between my own two ears. I had to adapt to what was, not the other way around.

Inside the country of KSA and outside the compound limits, the vast landscape of the desert contained different rules and standards that still existed after generations. In order to appreciate our surroundings I needed first to observe, study and learn. Fortunately, we met people on the compound who were willing to act as mentors or guides. Desert-savvy, with plenty of *wasta* (influence) and large networks of Saudi acquaintances, many established Aramcons were natural adventurers and cultural mentors to others. Many told stories handed down from expat generation to generation. We were the beneficiaries of decades of handed-down storytelling about the desert, and people were willing to adopt us, take us on mini-expeditions to educate us on where we had landed. All of this helped us make the thousands of tiny adjustments that were required to live there and be happy.

Outside the Bedouin tent in the desert, the requisite white Mercedes, small white Toyota pickup truck and a huge variety of satellite dishes were lined up on one side. *Could they speak to astronauts circling in the space station?* I wondered. The far side of the tent was a small, orderly compound with woven wooden fences housing dozens of tiny goats. Between our hosts' limited English and our very basic Arabic, we intuited our way through the process of being acceptable guests. We watched their ritual of getting to know us; yes, we were different, yet they were still welcoming. Our one common bond: curiosity about the other.

Very quickly, we were all laughing and smiling. The Saudis were talking to Lynsey, showing her the goats and asking if she had one! Apparently, we had arrived at the perfect moment. The goats were about to have their daily exercise. The elderly fellow opened the small compound gate, and literally more than a hundred small goats tumbled out en masse, running to who knows where, but clearly thrilled to be free. One of the most visceral and distinctive memories of my entire sojourn in Arabia was the sound of the pitter-patter of their tiny feet on the sand. The soft cacophony is something I have heard neither before nor since.

Sitting in the tent, I felt like an alien. The smell of Arabic coffee made with cardamom seeds floating in tiny cups, mixed with animal scents and possibly some sort of interesting perfume, was an unfamiliar cocktail for my nose.

Being physically close to people who were so strange and fascinating created a disturbing sense of wonder. While I was not going to be spending my days in a Bedouin tent, the journey of discovery and education around the rawness of the Bedouin lifestyle went a long way toward explaining exactly what was going on around me when I was back in the compound. In that one visit, I learned that no matter how much I adapted, I would never fully understand this exotic, foreign and fabulous culture. However, I could learn to accept the hidden intention of a warm welcome. Making sense of and understanding this strange experience would happen at some later date.

I learned to be solidly in the moment, mindful of their customs and careful about my behavior and demeanor. It felt like walking on eggshells at first, but eventually spending time with all sorts of Saudi people—from Bedouin farmers to sophisticated, highly educated and vision-driven leaders who were molding globalization through the burgeoning petrochemical industry—became normal.

To this day, the smell and feel of the Arabian desert is lodged somewhere inside me. This seems to be how adaptation works: it happens invisibly somewhere in the light and dark parts of our souls.

Neurobiology and neuroscience is now unravelling and describing this process.

ADVENTURE, ADJUSTMENT AND APPRECIATION

Although everyone arrived in Arabia, not all of us arrived well. I arrived with a boatload of expectations from other expat assignments. Having had the benefit of living overseas for almost eighteen years, including twelve in America, was sometimes an advantage and sometimes a disadvantage.

During my first journey to the Middle East in the late 1970s, when I worked as an employee for J Ray McDermott, I learned to speak Arabic conversationally, could find my way around the souk and had tons of fun as a single gal with an enormous community that welcomed us as if the purpose of that part of the world was to host a giant, continuous house party. My early assumption was that Arabia in the 1990s would be like Dubai in the 1970s. I believe this notion held me back, set me back and isolated me from lessons I needed to learn early on.

My international adventures started after moving from the super-friendly city of Glasgow, Scotland to a sophisticated and cosmopolitan London. My job as a junior member of Her Majesty's Foreign and Commonwealth Office took me to Yaounde, Cameroon, which for a young twenty-something was a wild adventure. This was the genesis of my adventures as an Adult Third Culture person, or ATCK (adult third culture kid). At the conclusion of my assignment in Cameroon, I moved back to London then onto to Dubai. Each of these places presented not only geographical changes but also enormous economic, social and cultural mountains to be conquered. Each ultimately schooled me in becoming a chameleon wherever I go. This skill sustains me, wherever I find myself. I am now much like a turtle carrying its home on its back.

A new community, colleagues and system had embraced me in Cameroon, Dubai and London, just as John had been embraced the day after our arrival in Ras Tanura. My vision of landing and being swept off our feet, immediately involved in many activities and hobbies in a few weeks, was mistaken. Many wives and families were OOK (out of Kingdom) on long trips for the Christmas holidays. There were two families across the street, but their kids were older. I was also adjusting to who the heck I was going to be. It seemed I was primarily a "dependent" like it said on all the papers (*And what was the job description for "dependent"?* I wondered), then John's wife and Lynsey's mum. My identity had been tossed in the air like confetti, and I was unprepared for where it landed.

We had to physically adapt in order to tolerate the brutal heat, dense humidity and strange weather patterns. Average temperatures in the summer can reach up to 119 degrees, and the thermometers officially stop working at that temperature because laborers cannot legally toil outside when temperatures go higher. Our work, play and social lives were all customized to the searing heat and the sand so prevalent in the air or under our feet.

Avoiding the heat of the day became the game. Our lifestyle patterns revolved around moving from blistering heat to icy air-conditioning in offices, cars and stores.

My ears had to accommodate Arabic in town and dozens of accents on camp. Listening to English, even as a native English speaker, takes more focus, concentration and mental gymnastics than we think when it is expressed by multiple nationalities. While a delight to the ears, it just plain took more energy and concentration. My Lebanese neighbor spoke English perfectly. I could understand her easily but had to lean in to listen and engage with her husband; my South African massage therapist spoke with a beautiful Afrikaans accent; my Sri Lankan houseboy spoke limited English but pronounced it perfectly. I considered all the sounds a gift to the ears.

We lived in two compounds and three houses over fifteen years. Each neighborhood brought differing nationalities, languages and influences to our attention. Our Saudi neighbor in Ras Tanura always invited me into her home at the drop of a hat. I think I was the token American/foreigner she wanted to show off to her Saudi friends, none of whom spoke a bit of English. I remember tea parties and family events. In stark contrast, another Saudi neighbor in Dhahran would look away or down when he encountered me outside. I adjusted. I learned this was neither personal nor rude. I made allowances; most times it was simply an unfamiliarity with Westerners, females or both and/or frequently a lack of confidence in the English language. It was clearly never all about me.

Foraging for food required us to adopt fierce shopping practices. It became like a black-belt preoccupation. Back then, because women could not drive, we were ferried to town by huge shoppers' buses that ran every day on a timetable that accommodated the constantly changing prayer times. There were precious minutes between arriving in town and prayer time, when shops abruptly closed. These large, comfortable coaches would disgorge about three dozen women to roam the streets, darting in and out of stores like veiled black ghosts. I learned the art of highly intentional shopping. We had to be physically prepared. Western toilets were a rare find downtown. One of the Welcome Ladies told me that she constantly prepared women for the bathroom scenarios they might find in town, even to the extent of demonstrating how to use an Eastern toilet, which several women declined to use to the point of suffering.

Foods were a delight to discover, and to this day our family misses the Afghani sugar bread in the town of Rahima and the cheese bread from Latifa Bakery. We miss celebrating Iftar and breaking the Ramadan fast with our Jordanian, Palestinian and Saudi friends. I long for dinners like those with multiple platters piled high with delicacies cooked in their home kitchens–what a joy and a party for all the senses.

NEW PLACE, NEW YOU AND ME

The multicultural influences we were subject to in Saudi shone a light on how alike we were. Every imported person on the Aramco compound had dreams, goals and motivation no matter our nationality, language or hereditary cultures. We bonded, built friendships and developed a new sense of family over conversations around those dreams. In our cul-de-sac in Dhahran, we would meet in the green space in the middle to celebrate our multiculturalism. This tiny corner of the world contained folk from Ireland, Chile, UK, US, Saudi, Finland and more. We shared each other's foods and celebrated Halloween and other traditions together. We were classic immigrants armed with intentions, dreams and energy.

Naturally there was a predominance of Western influence on the compound since so many of us were Brits, Americans or Canadians, not to mention Australians, South Africans and New Zealanders. We also enjoyed a healthy sprinkling of global perspectives represented by people from all around the planet. At the Pentecost service in the Anglican community, I remember twenty-three languages being spoken. That was a day to celebrate that we all do life differently influenced by our languages and our thinking; the key was to do it together with grace and hospitality.

People got married, gave birth to children and spent years raising them in this multifaceted soup. My partner in the Dhahran School yearbook, The Shamal, was a second generation Aramcon, having grown up in Arabia. One of her children was born in Arabia but could never be a Saudi citizen.

We were reinventing ourselves constantly. The possibilities were wide open in Aramco to enjoy new pastimes and to develop previously dormant skills and talents. A broad range of activities were offered, and with time, energy and interest on our side we could choose to become almost anything.

I witnessed engineers transform into indoor cycling instructors, dentists into salsa dance instructors, nurses into Tai Chi instructors after hours. Women who had previously been focused on raising children became café owners, gifted potters or accomplished actors. The facilities, equipment and time were available, and when people seized the day, they blossomed within the desert environment. I found myself inside a community that was brimming with aspiration, accomplishment and a hunger to grow on a personal level.

MAKING THE SWITCH

Our physical freedom was severely curtailed by the compound, which was entirely surrounded by a twelve-foot barbed-wire fence. Arriving or departing from the compound, we had to navigate the security gate, which consisted of a building with barriers and guards who checked everyone. Surprise, surprise, my freedom was suddenly, abruptly and unquestionably curtailed. I had imagined I was prepared for this, but nothing leading up to this moment prepared me for the turmoil, confusion and visceral sense of imprisonment of living in a cage of my choosing.

Learning to do what I could with what there was available was one of the first lessons presented to me. And, of course, there were was so much to explore inside the compound that I eventually managed to distract myself from the my preoccupation with fencing on one side, one of the most secure refineries in the globe to the south, the gulf on another and several levels of security barriers and gates on the fourth. My life felt like it was being managed by outside forces, way beyond my control, and I decided in an effort to build a sense of well-being for all three of us that I needed to button up any complaints or internal whining inside my head.

My personal life in Ras Tanura required making a daily decision to thrive. I needed to learn by focusing on what I could do and find joy in the middle of what felt like drudgery and doom for a few months. The beach was the saving grace in my adaptation process. I loved the beach.

There was one store, the Commissary, which was effectively a very large mini-mart that sold imported basic foodstuffs. The florist next door at that time would make a florist in the West roll over in their grave. A variety of silk plants and flowers, together with a minimal choice of fresh blooms, were available, although the state of the sad blossoms after a few days was a reminder that they were as displaced as the people who purchased them. Nevertheless, the florist was a great sign of normality, and having fresh flowers was the start of building a gratitude practice. I learned to be thankful for a beautiful imported pink lily on the edge of the vast Arabian desert. It was always the small things that made the difference. Next door to the flower shop was the mail center. Hundreds of neat boxes the likes of which you would find anywhere in a US mailing store were lined up. Kindly Filipino fellows supervised mailing packages, the sale of stamps and occasionally a few bureaucratic forms. I thought of it as a center of well-being. The people manning it were welcoming and friendly and for the most part had a terrific sense of humor. I made a note to self: *visit the mail center.*

Arriving in December meant that the weather was conducive to bicycling; however, our shipment from Japan with the trusted bicycle did not arrive until March when the intense heat started. I talked myself out of bicycling to get groceries.

LETTING GO

Becoming cheerful, open to change and relentlessly positive in the face of what felt like the "happy police" descending took daily practice for me.

The local Mutawa were the religious police that I had been warned about multiple times. They were fairly active in Rahima, the local town just outside the gates. Between the Mutawa, the women wearing abayas and the lack of entertainment, concerts or movies, I very much felt, initially, like all these circumstances were ways to thwart my personal happiness. In hindsight I was behaving like a spoiled bored housewife and not the adventurer I wanted to be.

After the fun stage of novelty and newness, the honeymoon was over. I was definitely in the trenches and realized that I needed to resolve the dilemma between the way I wanted life to be and the way it actually was. There were three major areas I needed to examine. The first was my hurry-up-and-get-it-done approach to life. I had to relinquish my perception of time. This desert kingdom, with its modulated approach and unrelenting marking of time by prayer calls, was going to involve a much larger adaptation and change than I had prepared myself for. Even in Dubai we had worked, shopped, eaten or driven during prayer calls; this was proving to be very different. Being patient pays off in the East, from sitting and drinking coffee when you enter a store to just being willing to hang around until you get the answer you really want.

The second was my expectations; I had to relinquish my perception that other Westerners thought like me. And the third was I had to learn that simply because my community of expats was a small one did not mean it was an easy community to maneuver inside.

STOP HURRYING

My introduction to Arabian patience was with one of my husband's colleagues in Japan, even prior to my arrival in Saudi. He wanted to lease a large family mover, a huge SUV by Japanese standards, for his Saudi wife, the maid and his six children. He went to the dealership and basically took an entire eight-hour day to bargain them down. We laughed when he told the story of taking several of the younger kids with him and the mayhem they created in the dealership while he calmly waited. This was an uncommon phenomenon in Japan, where their boundaries tend to be extremely fixed when it comes to prices. By basically waiting them out, he got the task accomplished without any of the stress or hurry that we Westerners often bring to a project. I was already being exposed to the forbearance that Arabs so readily practice.

Our very first weekend "in Kingdom" we decided to visit the big city, Al Khobar, which was about sixty miles distant. After checking maps, we walked to a bus stop only to find that the buses left from the recreation center and we had missed the only bus that morning. Undeterred, we found a number for a taxi, and a bearded elderly taxi driver, no less than seventy-eight years of age, in a dark *thobe* with his *ghutra* thrown back to one side of his face, showed up smiling from ear to ear. While his driving was erratic, we were hypnotized by the landscape and held tight to three-year-old Lynsey since there was no car seat or seat belt in sight. Our driver was entertaining. His mixture of Arabic and English—which we'd come to call "Arabish"—was charming, and my conversational Arabic from my time spent in Dubai came rushing back.

He dropped us off on King Khalid street. "La" (no), he could not wait for us; "la," he could not be called or summoned to pick us up. We found ourselves meandering from store to store, getting the feel for what would in the future be our stomping grounds. About an hour after our arrival, the shopkeepers started to turn out the lights and close the doors, and they invited everyone to depart in order that midmorning prayer could occur. We found ourselves on the streets with all restaurants and stores closed and people heading toward the mosque. We ruminated on what was possible and ran into some Western expats, who, it turns out, were from Ras Tanura. Upon requesting how to find a taxi to return us to the compound, they immediately invited us to travel with them. On the journey back we were treated to lists of tips, suggestions and lifestyle tweaks that we should make. Their open-hearted invitation and hospitality were the epitome of what we were to enjoy from then onward.

On camp, we were blessed to have a maintenance department. We could simply pick up the phone, dial 939 and a plumber, electrician or carpenter would show up to provide the service—at no cost, of course, except in terms of time. Frequently they would show up without the correct bulbs, tools or equipment necessary to complete the work, so it would languish for another few days. It often felt like a miracle when the talent, skills, personnel and tools all arrived in the same place and got the work accomplished.

I quickly learned to follow the pace of the system, to give up my sense of scheduling and hurriedness. In all our adventures, from being stuck up to our axles in sand in the desert to getting lost, we learned to remain calm and to look and see what solution naturally presented itself … hurry and scurry were disturbances in the force.

TIME AND THE CALENDAR

In Arabia, we lived in a different paradigm—one based on the position of the moon, a system that was established hundreds of years prior to our arrival. In the *Hijri* calendar a new month begins after an Islamic scholar has viewed the waxing crescent moon. This may seem a small detail, but in fact this system affects you to the core of your being.

There are twelve months like the Gregorian calendar, but only 354 or 355 days per year; therefore, adjustments between the two calendars are required. The Hijri calendar is not manipulated to follow the solar calendar. Since business is a global establishment, most Muslim countries practice business in the Gregorian system, but traditions, religious holidays and observances are all based in the Islamic system—a multilayered way to live.

The Islamic calendar is the basis for Shariah law, and while Saudi is the functional heart of Islam, it is also the focal point for all Muslims around the world to turn to five times per day. As a third of the planet faces Mecca when they pray, Saudi receives an inflated sense of respect that other Islamic countries do not enjoy and that Saudi takes very seriously.

While business is mostly conducted in the Western framework, offices opening at 7 a.m. and closing at 4 p.m., the natural cycles of life in terms of shopping, commerce, eating and sleep all revolve around the Islamic system. The combination of Hijri and the Western Gregorian calendar makes life interesting and sometimes comical in terms of kids getting out of school, husbands returning from work and shops being open for errands. It was really like a mad *Leave It to Beaver* experience in so many mysterious ways.

Prayer call echoes across the land upon the rising of the sun, and each prayer call that day occurs at a different time from the day before. In *Simple Gestures: A Cultural Journey into the Middle East*, Andrea B. Rugh describes juggling the concept of time during the

1960s. Back then they reset the clocks every single day just as the last sliver of sun dipped into the Red Sea. This was both imprecise and annoying, but necessary to align the Hijri calendar with Greenwich Mean Time (GMT). Dealing with two time systems, calendars and mindsets is a fact of life.

During my time in Saudi we were given a wallet size calendar with five prayer times for every day of the year. This would dictate the bus schedule into town and the times the shops would be open or closed. Nowadays this has turned into an app on the phone, by which you can organize and direct your errands, commercial activities and plans for the day. Without knowing prayer times, you would never know when a store or a restaurant might be open.

SIMILARITY TRAP

There seems to be a faction in all expat communities that takes pleasure in bashing the locals and their ways of being. In every country, critical or negative guys and gals congregate to complain. I needed to learn exactly who I would and should line up with and how to choose my friends carefully. Your choice of friends frequently shapes the journey when you are so far from home.

In the beginning I often found myself trying to squeeze into square-shaped holes when I was clearly a round person. One of my first havens was the group of Hatha yoga practitioners in Ras Tanura who met at a gal's house just behind mine. An example of seeking to belong where I didn't was in joining clubs with a bunch of girls I really enjoyed, but who had different backgrounds from me. Frequently, whether our backgrounds encourage fixed or growth mindsets ultimately makes the difference in whether we align with someone. Finding your real tribe, learning whom you truly belong with and whom you would *like* to belong with is a critical component of overseas life. Learning how to stay with the positive thinkers, the people who enjoyed having fun, the doers and the believers, was a lesson for me. This lesson applies also for the return journey, when you arrive back home and are once again rebuilding your connections and interests.

EXPECTATIONS: THE INVISIBLE BURDEN

Hidden expectations of other cultures and people are insidious and creep in when least expected. I had arrived with a hidden expectation that the Saudi women would be cowed, somewhat backward, oppressed and uncomfortable around foreigners, but to my surprise and delight my neighbor across the street in Ras Tanura was 180 degrees different from my expectations.

Her name was Adelmira, which means "the exalted one." Although she spoke very poor English, it was at that time way better than my Arabic. She invited me to her home many times, as I previously mentioned. I felt out of place and awkward initially, but with practice learned to relax, observe and generally enjoy the surprisingly high-spirited conversations and food. The women-only dancing was boisterous and exuberant; this was an enormous surprise to me. Her friends were highly curious about Westerners. Their perception of us was that we were all Kardashians. They imagined that we lived classic soap opera existences and were madly curious about our private, home and sex lives. Another jaw-dropping moment, when

Saudi women inquired about one's sex life. This occurred on a couple of occasions over my fifteen years in Kingdom—curiosity comes in all forms.

TIME, SIMPLE OR COMPLEX

Interestingly, much of my self-development work was based on many of the habits I saw practiced quite naturally by Saudis. How many times do we hear advice on not hurrying, being present or practicing mindfulness nowadays? And what an opportunity it was to live in a country that effectively stopped five times per day to reflect. Living at Saudi Aramco was almost like living on the monochronic scale, where people tended to do one simple task at a time, unlike the West on the polychronic scale, where it is common to see someone shopping, talking on their phone and drinking coffee all at once.

How frequently are we exhorted to be present to the use of our time? And how, after living in a polychronic society in the West, it was a treasure to live in a monochronic society and be subject to both systems of time and both ways of being. Choices of ways of being seemed to be open to all.

In Pico Iyer's TED talk, "Where Is Home?," the novelist said, "The beauty of being surrounded by the foreign is that it slaps you awake." While stories lingered with us, each day required that we firmly place them in the past so we could create the next chapter. I definitely remember a period of time where the combined influences of culture, language and physical realities were constantly slapping me awake.

All the while the steady drumbeat of living, working and

harmonizing with a vastly foreign culture was permeating our lives in ways seen and unseen. We could clearly see the differences in the food we ate at the Dining Hall and hear the call to prayer, but what ultimately were the invisible effects of this culture?

Humans are lit up by the novelty that travel offers our senses. Neuroscience reveals that over time, our brains are impregnated with a certain culture. It's almost like a culture literally rubs off on us. In the process, we learn about our own and the "other" identity, which can, if we are willing, lead us in understanding what it truly means to be, at our core, human.

Moving to a foreign culture involves massive change, and often the easiest portion to manage is the logistics: packing, bureaucratic paperwork and so on. I call this the "tip of the iceberg" for a move.

Saying farewell and goodbye to cultural perspectives, attitudes and prejudices that we carry like invisible garments can be challenging because we are unaware that we even own them. For the most part we end up in a new place with an old mindset, carrying hidden biases that we cannot even imagine exist. We go through life pretty much not knowing what we don't know. Until we come face to face with an entirely different way of living, we are not challenged to change our beliefs nor our perspectives. Spending time with others different from ourselves, can, if we are interested, help define what truly unites us and what clearly distinguishes us one from the other.

It was pure delight to be exposed to "others" who were also Westerners and "others" who were not. It was a constant delight to learn we are each unique, even with our commonalities, to have the opportunity to fraternize with so many nationalities and find at our core we were much more similar than we ever might have perceived.

How many times are we encouraged to invite diversity, include others unlike ourselves or practice intercultural interactions? If ever there was a laboratory in which to experiment with all of the above, Saudi Aramco was the perfect place.

Chapter 5

EMBRACING ALL OF IT!

I OFTEN TELL PEOPLE THAT LIFE is portable and you can take it with you wherever you go—just go. In order to be successful embracing a new reality it's important to first of all embrace flexibility, adaptability, adventure and optimism. An almost constant mindset of negotiation and curiosity carries us a long way on these international journeys.

PRIVILEGE

All personnel, whether Americans, Canadians, Brits, Filipinos, South Americans, Europeans, Indians, Bangladeshis or Sri Lankans, were on differing pay scales at Aramco. This stratification was originally designed to compensate people in relation to their standard of living back home. Housing was distributed according to grade codes and length of time served in Kingdom. The length of time served by old-timers or newbies was therefore visible in the type, size, and style of home. John spearheaded a new policy to design a different and perhaps fairer approach to pay scales at King Abdullah Petroleum Studies and Research Center (KAPSARC).

We as Americans were privileged to be top of the pile as it were. I felt like that brought along with it the responsibility of being sensitive to others less fortunate, to be crazy-generous and to participate in the circulation of wealth and goods to the absolute max. Living in daily gratitude for the lives we were experiencing compared to others was a major game changer for me. *There but for the grace of God, I could have been a Bangladeshi street sweeper, working outside in 112-degree weather,* I would frequently tell myself.

Off-camp, out on the economy (the real Arabia), there was a there was a even clearer class hierarchy. Arabs in beautifully tailored thobes of fine material, pressed and starched, with the quintessential status watch dominated. Westerners such as Americans, Brits, Europeans, Australians and Kiwis were just a hodgepodge of nationalities. A huge hierarchy no doubt operated between the Filipinos, Indians and Bangladeshis. Many of them had paid extraordinary prices for their visas, were paid very little and yet sent 80 percent of their money back to their homeland to support wives and children.

It took me a few years to realize that I was exactly like them—that I was merely a privileged version of the legal immigrants. There are many ways of being an immigrant. Although I was enjoying the luxuries of an urban American home, schooling for my daughter, traveling on passports that opened doors, speaking a dominant world language and a husband working at a highly professional level in an air-conditioned office, with cars and a dependable salary and all the status that entailed, at depth I was just like these people. I was living in Saudi to build a better life for our family. They were doing similarly without all the trappings and privilege.

MIXING HAVES AND HAVE-NOTS

Every day an army of workers who lived off the compound in barrack-like facilities would be bused to work as gardeners. They were outfitted in yellow, orange or blue jumpsuits, depending on the contractor. They would proceed to sweep every street, tend every plant, water and breathe life into every single bougainvillea bush. Their salaries were pitiful—we heard just a dollar or two per day. They worked outside in all weather, including in 110 degrees, pouring asphalt and working heavy equipment. We were cosseted and nurtured by their work, in that we enjoyed a beautiful environment in what would otherwise have been a tortured desert bereft of manicured beauty.

These workers were all men from Bangladesh, India or Sri Lanka and had sacrificed much to move to Saudi to earn money to send home to support their families. For the most part we expats were in awe of their sacrifice, aware of their painful conditions and grateful for their labor.

Frequently the gardeners would knock on our doors, with an empty two-liter plastic bottle in hand, requesting that we fill the bottle with sweet water for them to drink. The tap water around the compound was salty, brackish and not purified. I was always humbled and impressed by their attitude of gratitude. Here I was living in an air-conditioned villa with so many choices, while these men toiled in the sun all day long in horrific heat in order to send a paltry few dollars back to their families. Their superior language skills were evident, in that they spoke a little Arabic and English with their own native language plus several other dialects.

Jacque was shocked by the way laborers worked in the desert. There might be twelve to fifteen men living in a trailer with no windows and no AC. Sandals all lined up outside, little pieces of clothing hung on a makeshift washing line. They would go into town occasionally to purchase their only joy, cigarettes.

Carolyn reports, "I was always giving water, fruit or whatever I had to the gardeners." Vicci commented that if she ever reincarnated, she would choose to be a Saudi gardener working for Aramco, able to sleep in the air-conditioned stillroom or garage during the hot hours of the day, because although that was menial to us, for those men that was the height of privilege. Their presence alongside us, serving us and taking care of us served to remind us daily of the privilege we enjoyed as educated Westerners.

Frequently people offered them shelter in their garage when it rained, or it was extra hot and they needed a shady spot to sleep; gave them toys, clothing or anything we had left over or to spare. These small acts of kindness would never balance the scale of inequality that life seemed to have dealt them, but it sure gave me the experience of being generous and a big dose of the reality that existed in many other countries.

THINGS ARE RARELY THE WAY THEY SEEM

In the multicultural soup we swam, situations would frequently come up where we had to fill in the blanks or make up a story to make sense of the circumstances. Often the story did not match reality. Here is an example of an incident that could happen anywhere in the world, except that the cultural layers in Saudi add questions, intrigue and mystery to the entire process. Linda recalls an experience she had in the Dhahran Clinic. Her roommate was a Saudi lady. There was no human interaction between them and a sense of unease was evident during the first forty-eight hours. A curtain separated the beds; however, it did not drown out the noise and hubbub that ensued every evening when approximately twenty people from her roommate's tribe showed up to visit. This practice was par for the course and quite within acceptable limits for the Aramco clinic, where about 70 percent of the patients were Saudis. The energy level would skyrocket in the evenings while dozens of people would visit her Saudi roommate. The curtain between beds would be pulled back and Linda's one guest chair spirited away.

After a few days in the clinic, Linda decided she was not going to fret about the perceived rudeness and "lack of consideration." She chose not to engage and made a decision that this Saudi woman was unused to foreigners, spoke no English and was not Western-oriented.

Two more days of each behaving as if the other didn't exist went by. The day before Linda was released, she greeted her roommate with a polite "As-Salaam-Alaikum" on her way to the bathroom. A few minutes later the curtain between the beds was tugged vigorously. Her roommate sought to capture Linda's attention, and streams of

Arabic flowed toward her. The Saudi gal was trying desperately to return the salutation, as that is the cultural tradition, the ritual and the proper way to behave. Salutations and greetings are key moments in Arabic culture and set the tone for relationships. I also believe that they create a lovely system of respect between people that is absent in many Western relationships.

A conversation ensued, part Arabic and part English. This lady's name was Sarah, and she was in her mid-fifties to sixty with a family of nine children. Not one word of English appeared in Sarah's vocabulary; however, Linda had taken a few Arabic classes and with a lot of pointing and giggling, over the next twenty-four hours, a sweet cross-cultural relationship blossomed. Sarah had lost a seventeen-year-old son in a car accident and experienced a stroke herself on hearing the news. Her entire life had changed abruptly, so what Linda assumed was a negative attitude was in fact a mixture of shock, grief and lack of multicultural skills. Linda managed to connect the dots from a Western occupational therapist who explained that Sarah came from the village of Saihat and was probably a Shia, who are sometimes considered second-class Saudis by the Sunni population (which includes the ruling family).

As foreigners it was necessary to invent stories about why things were the way they were in Saudi, but when we had up-close and personal glimpses into individuals' lives we would frequently develop not only a charming relationship but also a quite different perspective.

BUS AS SOCIAL INSTITUTION

In Al-Hasa, a town about two hours from Dhahran, there was a remote clinic operated by Aramco and staffed with a multinational workforce. The closest camp to Al-Hasa was an Aramco-sponsored compound called Udhailiyah, where many expats lived and worked. Michelle lived in Udhailiyah and worked in the clinic in Al-Hasa. Company buses would drive through the villages and collect Saudi employees then deliver them to work. The bus drivers were typically Filipinos who were reliable and congenial. The buses would drive circular routes several times each day.

The Aramco bus became a social networking system for some local Saudi women. Each day villagers would pack a picnic, board the bus, go to the clinic and basically hang out all day long. This was their social outing for the day. The buses and clinic actually facilitated village social life. Most of these gals were fully veiled wearing hot, stuffy abayas. Entertainment consisted of visiting with their friends and watching all the patient and staff comings and goings. They appreciated the free transportation, clean running water and air-conditioning. Lunch consisted of flasks full of hot tea or Arabic coffee, bread and cookies.

One day the most popular socialite from the community was missing. Michelle noticed this woman's absence and questioned the regular Filipino bus driver as to her whereabouts. He replied, "Oh, she is sick today; therefore, she won't be coming to the clinic." They laughed together at the irony of it all.

SHOPPING

One of my husband's first shopping experiences was in downtown Al Rahima, a small town near the Ras Tanura compound. He was looking for an electrical appliance and found that he had to walk around a rather large crowd of Saudis who were watching a TV set in the window of the store.

On emerging from the store, he got curious and navigated the crowd to secure a better view. He was flabbergasted that they were watching Billy Graham, a fundamental Western Christian preacher, holding forth and preaching the gospel of Jesus. Apparently, the crowd was enthralled.

My first shopping experience on the compound in Ras Tanura was when I spotted a large truck laden with fruit and vegetables parked outside a neighbor's house. I immediately marched over to discover two Indian brothers selling their goods. I remember being thrilled to find lemons from Lebanon, mangoes from India and kiwis from Sri Lanka; this was literally a global fruit basket on wheels.

This truck became the primary provider of all our fruit and vegetables for six years. After bagging my choices, they would politely carry the bounty into the kitchen and place it right on the counter. I noticed I was always more grateful for the service and the foods than I am in a grocery store back home. I loved the sense of simplicity, the ease and grace we were privileged to observe. We also were relieved of concerns regarding Monsanto and GMOs. Because the produce came from around the globe, we had to throw concern to the wind and simply receive, be grateful and eat well. Sadly, after 9/11, the fruit men ceased coming. We were told that they did not fulfill the new security rules, so they were no longer permitted on camp. I often look back on that shopping experience with great longing.

Another perennial colorful character was the "fish man," who would show up at the house in a battered and beaten old truck laden with coolers of amazing fresh fish. His unique value-added proposition was delivering fresh produce directly from the sea. Not only would he sell the shrimp, hamour or red snapper, but he would come into the kitchen, hijack one's sink and start peeling and cleaning the fish. He varied from being grumpy to feisty and funny. Speaking broken English, he basically commandeered the kitchen, demanding specific equipment. I laughed and let him get on with the task.

And then there was Tex, practically an institution in his own right. Tex was a Saudi who grew up in Texas in the seventies. He traveled door to door around the compound with artifacts: old Yemeni or Bedouin jewelry, amazing pots, old rugs, samovars—and a Texan accent as big as his truck. He showed up with a driver and would march into the house with armfuls of junk or treasure. Over the years thousands of Aramcons have become the owners, custodians and beneficiaries of various and sundry pots, old knives, ancient jewelry, doors and window frames, which now decorate their homes and remind them of their other home in Saudi.

Lots of treasures and fun experiences were gleaned in the markets and souks. Souks were full of wonder and amusing items that either tickled or puzzled my Western mind, and they made life easy, as they were essentially groupings of similar stores. There are souks devoted to gold, spices, electrical items, kitchenware, clothing and household goods. One friend found a perfume called Viagra when shopping in the very old city of Hofuf. There were multiple "fix-it" stores. My favorite watch store handled all the major luxury brands, and everything could be repaired in a couple of days. We formed personal relationships with people, like Abdullah the watch repairer, Mohammed the tailor and another Mohammed from Pakistan who repaired our shoes. (Everything got repaired and/or recycled.)

After years of exploration, my personal favorite became the kitchen souk, which was run by a tall willowy Saudi fellow who perennially wore dark glasses and reminded me of Geordie in the *Star Trek: The Next Generation*. Piles of pots and pans were stacked as high as the ceiling. They even spilled out onto the sidewalks where dozens of teapots, kettles and coffee pots—from primitive to modern in every size, shape and color—seemed to reflect the basic Saudi value of hospitality. To this day my kitchen reflects the contents of these stores.

Shopping was limited to stealing short windows of opportunity between prayers, meals and after sleep basically. The average shopping day would be relegated to getting on the 9 a.m. bus. When our girls were little, my friend and I would take our four-year-olds down to the bus in the morning. Frequently the merchants would hand them sample perfumes or a little set of brass cups and saucers and other miniature goodies that produced delight and surprise from the girls.

The buses would take us to either Al Shulah mall downtown or the Al Rashid mall, a large, shiny facility which opened soon after our arrival. Sadly the Al Shulah mall burned down in 1996. The streets around King Khalid Street were our primary stomping grounds. We came to know the shop owners by name; they were warm, friendly, gracious and welcoming. If we arrived early in the morning we would often score a wonderful little gift, a *baksheesh*, since their tradition states that making the first sale of the day is an omen of success, and ritual requires that you give generously by giving back, like paying it forward.

Prior to 9/11, getting ready to go shopping meant dressing

relatively modestly with arms and legs covered with loose, flowy garments. During the "reign of terror" years, security became a much greater issue, and we were asked to show our ID cards upon getting on a bus, so the driver could be absolutely certain we were bona fide Aramcons. The other major shift was in how we dressed. In the eighteen months after 9/11, more and more Westerners could be found wearing the abaya downtown and in the malls.

This was a very personal decision. No one told us to wear one, and to my knowledge no one suggested or requested we wear one. If they had, there would have been an outcry. As a matter of personal choice, I started wearing the abaya because I could wear no sleeves and a pair of exercise pants underneath it, which gave me a sense of freedom. My primary focus was to avoid attention. A conversation could frequently be heard between the old-timers who had lived in Kingdom for decades and the newbies who had just arrived and were doing their best to "follow the rules," except the rules were never one-hundred percent clear.

WHEREVER THE PETS ARE—HOME IS

Prior to arriving in Arabia I had a conversation with a friend already in Kingdom about the possibility of us getting a pet. Having had a miscarriage while on the short assignment in Japan, I had the notion that we needed to heal, and a pet would be an important addition. Our adage had always been "home is where the pet lives."

My friend Mary did some great research and recommended we contact the Ras Tanura local Kennel Club, which was staffed by a Western vet a day or two per week, upon arrival in Kingdom. Mary had discovered that puppies were going to be born in Ras Tanura and the family would be looking for homes.

On a bright and early Christmas morning, a real live Western Santa Claus rang the doorbell carrying a crate with a huge gold bow with red trim (which we still have). Inside was a wriggling bundle of puppy energy. Lynsey was overjoyed and for a lifetime convinced that Santa Claus is for real. The puppy received a Japanese name, Satchi, in honor of our time in Japan.

About ten weeks after we arrived in Kingdom, Ramadan started. We had been prepped during orientation and by neighbors and friends upon arrival and were well aware of the rules. It is considered extremely bad form to eat or drink in the presence of someone participating in the fast. Foods were not to ever be eaten outside, and even in the corporate offices one had to be circumspect about drinking from the water fountains.

One morning upon returning from our regular walk I bent down to remove Satchi's leash prior to opening the front door to our home. Just at that moment, the young Saudi fellow who lived across the street emerged from his house and headed toward the bus, his thobe billowing with the wind. In the split second before I opened the door, Satchi caught a glimpse of him and bolted as fast as his tiny legs would carry him.

When the young Saudi neighbor caught sight of the dog chasing him, he took off, which, of course, lured Satchi into believing he was involved in the best game of chase ever. There we were, a strange parade of a twelve-year-old Saudi boy chased by a small black furry ball with brown ears and me, a forty-something Western woman, in hot pursuit.

All I could think was, *It's Ramadan. Are dogs bad luck during Ramadan? Is this kid really terrified of little dogs? What the heck is happening here?* The kid arrived at the bus stop as the bus arrived and leapt through the air into the bus. Fortunately Satchi was too short to jump onto the bus, and while he danced around on his tiny back legs, I scooped him up to shuttle him back into the safety of our four walls. It took me some time to process the incident.

Eventually I shared the story in the Commissary with another expat, who explained that while many Arabs tolerated dogs and on occasion would keep them as status symbols, the majority of Muslims saw dogs as impure or dirty. If Satchi had touched our neighbor, he would have had to perform ablutions to cleanse himself prior to prayer. Thus, the flight response.

Clearly there were historical and cultural belief systems built up over hundreds of years that were all brought to the surface by a small incident. Usually it's the tiny behaviors that bring the invisible beliefs to light. One of my first cultural sensitivity lessons was that in order to maintain harmony with the local population, I would need to control my dog at all times.

And yet, a similar incident occurred ten years later while living in Dhahran. A well-spoken, Western-dressed Pakistani taxi driver come to the door to collect one of us for a journey downtown. Satchi bounded to the door and attempted to bestow his enthusiasm upon this hapless driver. The fellow took one look and took off, goose-stepping all the way around our cul-de-sac.

I always regretted both these incidents. They really demonstrated the programming that our cultures have around animals and beliefs relating to custom, tradition and religion.

Yet there are exceptions to every rule, and just when I would come to understand something was not quite a stereotype but more like a traditional behavior, I would be proved wrong. In fourth grade, Lynsey had the opportunity to write a paper on salukis, a beautiful type of sighthound who hunt by using their sight rather than scents. Historically they were carried on camels and used by the Bedouin to catch game animals. Frequently people alluded to the fact that they might have been treated better than women. Salukis can run at recorded speeds of up to forty-two miles per hour. It was not uncommon for expats to fall in love with the breed and bring several salukis back home with them.

The community and compound sheltered hundreds of Arabs from many different nationalities and backgrounds, and one of the invisible barriers was their perspective on dogs. Many times we would be out walking with two dogs and be approaching a Saudi couple dressed in traditional garb of thobe, ghutra, abaya and niqab. Our instinct would be to shorten the leashes and keep the dogs away from them unless they made an active move to engage with us or the dogs. Many would engage, but one never knew what the reaction would be.

One day Lani was out walking with her beautiful golden spaniel. A Saudi couple were walking toward her, and the fellow started to holler and wave his hands in the air, gesticulating that she stop. Her reaction was, *Oh, here we go again, more Saudis who hate dogs.* However as she got closer she discovered there was a scorpion in the path and the Saudi fellow was seeking to protect her dog from danger. How easy it was to jump to conclusions, pigeonholing each other on the basis of previous encounters. A conversation ensued and a British fellow on the way past in a golf cart grabbed a club and took care of the scorpion while the Saudi couple petted and cooed over Lani's dog.

Whether a Saudi would react to a pet, or whether they wore traditional or Western dress or if in fact they were practicing a behavior based on custom, tradition or religious belief was often a mystery.

In actual fact there was a terrific culture of support for the animals on the compound since Aramco hired two foreign vets to supervise the Kennel Club and offered services to all residents. We were the beneficiaries of those vet services throughout the care and keeping of four dogs and two horses.

FOODS—MISSING IN ACTION

In the eight decades of expatriates living in the Kingdom, food has naturally been a major topic of concern. I lived in Dubai in the 1970s alongside Aramcons who worked in Saudi. Dubai was more open and had greater trade and apparently more choices of foods. It always amused me to see the stocks of granola bars that the Aramcons would hoard and carry back to the Kingdom. Also during that period there were rules regarding supplies.

Before this, in the late 1960s, lettuces were rare and they were rationed. Helen reports being able to purchase only one lettuce per person. She would send her husband, son and houseboy to the Commissary as well in order to snag four lettuces for a large dinner party. It used to be common to have several friends purchase a missing item to contribute to a dinner party. Of course, in the spirit of what goes around, comes around, this would be reciprocated later.

We commonly called each other when we found goodies, like peanut butter or canned pumpkin in the Commissary or downtown, especially after the advent of cell phones. It is still common for staples to be missing. When we returned in 2015 we discovered that the Mexican restaurant was out of corn chips due to some snafu with the distribution system; however, they were available four blocks away in the Commissary so people just brought them to the restaurant.

If you live in Anywhere, USA, you've probably not experienced your local grocery store running out of everyday items like canned green beans or frozen spinach. If it does happen, you can usually go a mile away to another store for them. Shopping for groceries in the Dhahran area, however, was sometimes a challenge.

Someone would go to the Commissary in Dhahran and discover that a new shipment of Raisin Bran cereal had arrived. The average shopper would buy a couple of boxes and telephone their friends with the good news so they could do the same. It was considered a common courtesy.

Think about that. Getting excited about a box of cereal? Really? But, if it is your favorite and you have not tasted it in a year, you will certainly be excited.

There were others who would walk into the Commissary and "buy the whole shelf." They'd take the entire stock home and not tell friends because they might ask to buy a box and that would start the leaking of the news about their stash. Also, if the neighborhood kids ate breakfast with your children on the weekend, the last thing you would do is let them know that you had Raisin Bran. You would serve everyone Cheerios, which was always in stock at the Commissary.

The Dhahran Commissary and the Al Khobar/Dammam

grocery stores did their share of bringing in products that various nationalities desired, especially us Americans. One week they would have three different kinds of granola bars from the USA and then not have any at all for the next two months. Cindy reports that she was always surprised at the thought process of stocking the shelves. They would bring something in that the expats would really like so sell out quickly. She would ask, "When will you be getting this back in stock?" To which they would reply, "We will not reorder this because it sold out too quickly."

We shoppers had to be on our toes, and if we wanted to get news about what was new in stock, we had to be one of those who shared what we knew from our trips to the grocery store.

"There was a time when all of Saudi Arabia decided tampons were not healthy and there was not one in sight," Lisa reports. "Also chocolate was removed from company snack stands at the offices because it was considered unhealthy. That naturally didn't last long since many secretaries must have their chocolate, and we all know who runs a company." So true.

Carol recalls the time she purchased colored marshmallows for a sweet potato casserole. Imagine her surprise when she discovered that the coloring was also flavoring! Julia reports watching a few of the local Saudi women in the jelly aisle. They were trying to figure out what the jars contained. Julia watched one of the gals stick her finger in a jar, taste it, recap and replace it on the shelf. From then on, Julia would never buy jam without testing that the cap was on tight and, hopefully, had never been opened.

FOR THE LOVE OF FOOD

Hoarding groceries was a way of life for some in Dhahran. But Sharon took hoarding to the next level. Rob and Sharon spent more than twenty-five years in Dhahran. Sharon's lifetime favorite food is Mexican. She could eat it three meals a day, every day. She bought refried beans by the case, just to be sure. When she found really hot jalapeño peppers, she bought the whole shelf. When there were fresh flour tortillas, the grocery cart was filled and they were taken home and carefully repackaged and frozen. During Sharon's years in Dhahran, she made some really great Tex-Mex dishes for the dinner parties she hosted.

There were many American-based fast food franchises in the Dhahran/Al Khobar/Dammam area. However, at first there were none that leaned toward Tex-Mex food like Chipotle or Del Taco. In the 1990s, a rumor spread that Taco Bell was going to open a restaurant in Al Khobar. Then, one day, a friend called Rob and told him they saw a new place under construction and they were putting up a Taco Bell sign. Finally!

On opening day Sharon was one of the first to eat there. On the weekends, Rob and Sharon ate lunch at Taco Bell and carried extra home for the evening meal. A couple of times during the week, they ordered Taco Bell to be delivered. Yes, delivered. And the delivery guy loved to deliver to Sharon's house because he knew a nice tip awaited him.

One year, Sharon arranged for one of the staff to sell her one of their uniforms, complete with apron and cap, all with the Taco Bell logo. She was a hit at the Halloween party.

This routine went on for years. But, as in most things in the expat lane, good things come to an end. One evening during a visit to Taco Bell, one of the workers came and sat with Rob and Sharon for a minute or two. He looked around and quietly said, "We are not supposed to tell anyone, but the restaurant is closing at the end of the month when we finish our supplies. We do not know why, and management is not telling us."

Needless to say, Sharon was devastated. On the way home, she laid out her plan to Rob. Rob listened to the plan and replied with a very confused, "Huh?"

The following day found Rob in Al Khobar buying a freezer, which was delivered to their house in Dhahran. He also went to every cookware store until he found a food vacuum-sealer packaging machine. In true hoarding style, he bought all the plastic sealable bags they had in stock.

Over the next few weeks, Rob and Sharon made almost daily trips to Taco Bell or got home delivery. On the first trip and first order, Sharon said, "I'll take twenty-five bean burritos, twenty-five hard shell tacos with beans and twenty-five Mexican pizzas with beans, all for takeout." It took the staff by surprise, but they got busy. Another order for dine-in was placed while the crew worked on the large order.

At home, everything was vacuum-sealed in plastic bags and placed in the freezer. Rob and Sharon repeated this routine until the freezer was full. A last meal was eaten at Taco Bell to say goodbye to the staff and life went on. Rob says he had nightmares about the packaging of Taco Bell for a very long time.

As time went on, Sharon would go to the freezer on a special occasion and get a few burritos, tacos and maybe a Mexican pizza.

The food was dressed up with tomato, onion, lettuce, cheese and sour cream. The guests would inevitably say, "Hey, this taco looks and tastes like Taco Bell." Sharon would say, "That's because it is."

Taco Bell finally opened again in Al Khobar in 2012, a few years after Sharon's departure from Saudi Arabia. Hopefully, it will stay open to the Tex-Mex "closet eaters" for many years to come!

Allowing the adventure to be the teacher is part of a wonderful process of building trust. I would say any time we get to live with discomfort, by choice, there is always a silver lining to be gained.

Chapter 6

LIVING WITH DISRUPTION

ON JUNE 25, 1996, I was home on the idyllic compound of Ras Tanura. The perennial tranquility of that sleepy place broke with a shattering thud. Windows flexed, then settled back in place and a muted stillness emerged out of the ether, followed by a mind full of questions.

Our compound was attached at the southern end by way of stout security gates to the Ras Tanura refinery, which processed approximately 550,000 barrels of oil per day. The impact felt thunderous underfoot. I was very aware in that moment that a bunch of petroleum engineers, many of whom were now neighbors, were playing with dangerous chemicals within a mile of the house. I was also conscious that my husband's team was placing vessels that would be processing potentially explosive chemicals in the refinery.

Nevertheless, this felt very distant—it did not seem local.

We were living in an isolated world, void of cell phones, Facebook or emails and only limited television. The CNN cameras had departed after the drama of the Persian Gulf War. Waiting was my only option. An hour later, John called to let me know about an explosion at Khobar Towers—an unfamiliar name to me at that moment. Over the next five days more details emerged.

THE TERROR TICK-TOCK

The Khobar Towers housed about 2,000 US military personnel who worked at the King Abdul Aziz Air Base fifty miles away and patrolled the no-fly zone in southern Iraq, created at the end of the Gulf War just five years before. There were nineteen deaths of US servicemen on June 25 and almost 500 people, a mixture of civilians, contractors and military personnel, injured in the explosion. Many were transported to the company clinic for treatment in Dhahran.

This was the first major attack in the neighborhood since a Scud missile from Iraq landed in US Army barracks near the Toy Town mall in Dhahran, on February 26, 1991. That incident killed twenty-nine soldiers and injured more than 100 people during the Gulf War.

After Khobar Towers I discovered Warden Messages. These missives are written and distributed by local American Embassies and Consulates. They inform US citizens about potential threats and recommended behaviors to manage them. They often start with, "The US Embassy in Riyadh, the Consulate General in Dhahran and the Consulate General in Jeddah request that wardens pass the following message in its entirety to the US citizen community." Each area or conclave of expats had a person who would coordinate with the embassy to get the news out. After Khobar Towers and until we departed in 2010, we would receive a notice several times a week that said something like: "Due to the continuing risk of terrorist attacks by Al-Qaeda in the Arabian Peninsula across the Kingdom, the United States Mission in Saudi Arabia reiterates its recommendation that US citizens exercise caution in places frequented by foreigners." On the day of the Khobar Towers bombing, the level of the alert was low. This peaceful sense of well-being was going to be threatened frequently up until 2004, when the Oasis incident occurred and finally it seemed more decisive security measures were taken.

GROUND ZERO?

On September 11, 2001, I stood on one leg in the kitchen at the stove, stirring dinner with a wooden spoon. Our TV was on and I was watching the morning news on CNBC at our home on Nomad Trail in Dhahran. It was 5:43 in the early evening. After many years of wonky and intermittent TV service, peppered with Arabic music and pictures of the king receiving various dignitaries in long lines, we finally, oh joy, had access to regular US programming in the form of CNN and the *Today* show, which I would watch in the early evening. *Good Morning America* had quickly become a staple and was connecting us back to life in the US and around the globe in a way that delivered a sense of normality and balance missing for me up until then.

I, along with half the globe, watched as reality unfolded into the event now known as 9/11. Shock and dismay crept up my spine as we watched in real time as the second plane hit.

Within fifteen minutes my phone rang. I will never forget my friend Teresa wisely commenting, "This world will never ever be the same again." I felt a visceral lurch in my gut, and streams of alarm shot through my body as part of a response to this event back in my recently adopted "home" country. *If planes were being flown into buildings, how could we ever go back home ... it would take a plane to get there,* was my first thought. The feeling of isolation, being cut off and wondering what was happening, was similar to what every person around the world wondered. How strange the fleeting thoughts are that pass through one's mind during a flight or fight reaction. Many of us wondered, *Are we safe here? If there is an organization called Al-Qaeda, are they really here in Saudi; even more worrisome are they on the compound? Are they my neighbor? If they are my neighbor, how would I know this?"*

Al-Qaeda operatives were indeed discovered nearby eventually and were immediately spirited away, according to the rumor mill. *Were we living at ground zero—were we close to the genesis of all this violence? And if we were close, how close were we?* All these thoughts were running around inside me.

One-hundred percent of the Saudi people I had met and had interactions with, up until then, had been delightful, mostly because I rarely if ever saw the dark or extremist side and even out in the community enjoyed pleasant exchanges with the locals.

Investigations quickly revealed that several of the perpetrators were possibly from the Kingdom. This immediately threw an entirely different spotlight on the situation. Shock and mental confusion were my first responses to this. The massive organization that is Saudi Aramco Security went into action; I assumed they were intervening on our behalf. Extra guards were visible, particularly around the school. My friend Jane taught at the elementary school in the Hills. On day one after 9/11 she had bus duty. As the buses arrived at the school and disgorged their precious cargo of kindergartners through fifth graders, Aramco security guards were very much in evidence; up until then Security had behaved like any terrorism was simply mischief and therefore background noise. Jane says, "Everyone showed up at the school feeling like they had been punched in the stomach." Administrators, teachers, aides and all the adults arrived with the same preoccupation. As the kids started getting off the bus, a very grandfatherly Saudi guard, Ahmed, with a long beard and typical compassionate disposition, walked up to Jane, pointed to the sky and brought his fingertips together in a symbol of prayer and simply kept repeating, "Same, same, one God-your-God-my God–your children–my children." Essentially his message was, "I care about these children like my own and I am here to protect them."

Buried in that statement was the heart and soul of most of the Saudi people. Here was a Saudi telling an American that although a great crime had been committed on home soil in the US, he personally felt connected to us and was willing to do his part to protect our kids if called to do so. Jane shared with me what a powerful experience this was for her. This expression of sympathy was common from Saudis we knew and went a long way to calming our anxieties.

Ann had developed a kindly relationship with the Saudi supervisor of the gardening department on camp after her arrival. He seemed to take a personal interest in her garden. Shortly after 9/11,

Mohammed showed up at her house, rang the front doorbell and stood on the doorstep wringing his hands. He came to apologize if she was experiencing any pain or fear as a result of the behavior of his fellow citizens. The sentiment seemed sincere and deeply heartfelt. Ann was very touched by this.

Anxieties remained, however. A pall fell over the entire community. Westerners kept their heads down and for the most part didn't mention the situation in the office. At gatherings of expats in the Dining Hall for lunch, they kept their tone moderate, acted as if nothing had happened and paid close attention to their surroundings.

Many witnessed Saudi colleagues who appeared to be gloating or celebrating, as if with glee that the US had suffered. Although there were reports that a few Saudis were secretly celebrating the events of 9/11, I personally never experienced that. Urban myths or just gossip included stories of female Saudi dentists in Riyadh who held a party to celebrate 9/11 and ordered cakes baked in the shape of the twin towers, although it's entirely possible they were already holding a party and this was simply a creative idea they came up with—we will never know. Reports emerged of entire departments where Westerners were shunned for a few weeks. It was entirely likely that unskilled intercultural interactions were rising to the surface. Humans are not programmed to be perfect. Everyone was managing as best they could.

Other departments endured stoicism and behaved as if they had just read the British World War II poster "Keep Calm and Carry On". Some expats were found huddled together in cubicles comparing notes and closely monitoring reaction on the part of Arabs around them. It was common for a Western expat to be the only Westerner in an office, and many told me that it was an isolating time period where banter between cultures subsided, and there was a definite cooling in some relationships.

Jacque was an administrator with the Drilling Group, working closely with Western drillers and Saudi management. On September 12 she went to work as usual, the only Western female working with a group of intelligent, Western-educated Saudi males. Years later Jacque recalled those days for me.

"I have to say it was the quietest week," she recounts. "People would not look at you, nobody talked about it, no one looked at each other. It was business as usual only with a very uneasy feeling; everyone was processing and awaiting more information."

She emphasized how positive her professional work experience had been with that particular group. "The Saudi men I worked with were very respectful, more than any group of men I have ever met. They did not look directly at me very often, although they appeared polite and kindly, unlike some of the US and Canadian drillers," she says" As foreigners we were concerned for our physical well-being. *If there was such a coordinated effort against the West, would we be turned into soft targets?* The fact that Saudis were implicated was stunning to us. Mostly we enjoyed a collegiality between our cultures."

Jacque wondered what her American family and friends were going to say about her remaining in Kingdom. "Were they going to criticize me for working, making money? And how would they view me after that?" She was extremely philosophical and focused on the lessons she took from this experience. "You are very much the product of your life path. If friends and family back home want to criticize us—fine." For many it took a rebellious attitude and some courage to choose the road less traveled and to remain in Kingdom after 9/11.

Throughout the offices, at the Commissary and around the compound in general were whispered conversations where Saudis would mumble, "We don't understand," "We are just as confused as you are," "These are not People of the Book," and "This is a deviation—not natural; this is not who we are or who we want to be known as." Several of my friends and I had Saudi women approach us in the malls expressing their confusion and disorientation around these events. They seemed so sincere and benevolent that I felt inclined to believe they had nothing but good intentions; otherwise they would not normally have approached us.

Despite our mostly positive interactions in the local community, many extremists and traditional locals believed that while the US essentially rescued Arabia during the Gulf War, their beliefs and their religion along with traditional practices had been steamrolled in the process, and their values had been crushed. Our countries shared common interests, but we did not necessarily share common values, and this period shone a light on the difference.

THE FEAR THAT FOLLOWED

A small campaign of insurgency commenced in Saudi in November that year, possibly emboldened by the crisis that was 9/11. Car bombings and the occasional act of terror occurred. On the compound, it was easy to be cavalier and write these off, saying, "Well, if you lived in the middle of LA, you would never visit so-and-so neighborhood, so just stay on the compound." We developed an entire vocabulary of justifications around staying put. Travel warnings, threat alerts, warnings about leaving the compound and going out in public began to be daily fodder, not just an occasional "watch your back" sort of communiqué, and they became more threatening and specific.

Our questions, anxiety and discomfort grew, as did security, which we saw being beefed up daily in the most unexpected ways. Our little bubble of beautiful, peaceful and idyllic well-being had suddenly burst. A frequent concern one heard voiced at the time was that if the perpetrators were Saudi, was it possible that any woman wearing an abaya was suddenly a threat? Who was really under that abaya? A man or a woman? And what were they carrying?

We rarely went into town. For the most part we isolated ourselves on the compound while seeking to maintain the appearance of normalcy at home. All our energies were directed toward ducking—living under the radar and almost hibernating.

My friend Leova went to downtown Al Khobar on the bus one evening after work with an Irish gal, a coworker at the clinic. They were walking down King Khalid Street. Two Westerners walked toward them and passed them, and everyone continued their progress. Within about 35 seconds they suddenly experienced an enormous boom. The pavement shook; they turned around and were faced with an explosion fifty to seventy feet away. Body parts were flying through the air amid the acrid smell of burning flesh. The women instantly reacted with shock, grabbed each other and ran down a side street. A cab picked them up, and they piled into it holding onto each other the entire trip back to camp. A car bomb had gone off, and one of the Westerners they had just passed was killed in the blast, while the other was critically injured. Leova and her friend had just experienced a near-miss. Although this was a one-off experience, there was a series of events like this over several months.

Questions that would never have occurred to us a few months prior suddenly became top-of-mind problems. We worried and fretted about our safety and specifically the safety of our children. Bin Laden had not only killed 3,000 people and damaged New York, but he had damaged the faith and trust between nations, cultures and neighbors. We lived in three homes while in Saudi. In every location we had Saudi neighbors who lived, slept and ate within twenty yards of us. How could we possibly view them as dangerous or threatening and manage a stable life? We could not afford the indulgence of ever thinking that we were possibly in danger from our neighbors, colleagues or Saudi friends. A trip to downtown Al Khobar became unavoidable. It was my first visit to town after several weeks of holing up on the compound after 9/11. I was hyper-alert. I scrutinized every abaya-ed woman moving toward me. The first thing I would observe was her feet. This was a tip from a Saudi family we met while we were in Japan. They taught us that when a Saudi child becomes detached from his mother in the supermarket, looking up at black abayas is never useful. The child looks at the feet. He knows his mother's feet, their shape, size and shoes.

I applied this trick a lot. On King Khalid Street I found myself walking toward a broad-shouldered, hefty-looking fully-covered person with big, wide, clunky feet. I was doing my best to evaluate the walk, because Saudi women do not walk in an up and down manner like Westerners—they sail across the pavement. I remember thinking, *Am I being paranoid? Those feet look like a man's feet—what incendiary device might he be carrying under that abaya?* I rapidly ducked into an alley and wove my way through the gold souks, not turning around until I was several blocks away. Was my anxiety taking over my thoughts and behaviors? Or was this just the normal reaction to such strange circumstances?

Intercultural communication with all sorts of others who are of different faiths and beliefs and cultures requires extra energy at the best of times. Practicing mindfulness with Saudi people, being careful around women who were veiled and covered from head to toe, while managing my own head trash, elevated my focus, and I believe forever sharpened my intuition. Although I had worked in diplomatic missions and been trained in observation techniques, I delved even deeper. I learned to listen to the body language underneath the abaya. I learned to sense people, to feel them out instead of practicing a reactionary form of judgment. This took time and persistence. This one skill really served to make life acceptable, to manage the anxiety that sometimes wanted to bubble up and take hold.

While we watched the political analysts and observers describe the events in New York as a Saudi quarrel that happened to occur on US soil, we wondered what that meant in practical terms to us Westerners living on Saudi soil. Were we starting to see a crack in the façade of extremism? Were we watching the unfolding of a new era in Arabia? Were we in fact witnesses to the ushering in of a new mindset? What were we witnessing? And were we so involved by living there that we simply could not analyze the situation well? It is difficult to view the picture if you are in fact part of the frame.

THE SECOND IRAQ WAR AND BEYOND

From September 2001 until March 2003 this low level of terrorism continued. The second Iraq War officially began on March 17, 2003. On May 13 there was an immediate reprisal in the form of terrorist attacks on compounds in Riyadh. Was the Kingdom about to be dragged into the war? Were we to be living amid some sort of proxy war? These were our top-of-mind questions.

From March to November 2003 there were approximately thirty to forty deaths in Kingdom, with over 300 people injured in four major terrorist incidents. This was followed by six large incidents during 2004 in which about twenty people were killed and almost fifty injured. Cars exploded, people were shot, suicide bombers targeted the Saudi General Directorate of Traffic in Riyadh and gunmen burst into industrial complexes in the city of Yanbu. From coast to coast chaos was erupting and seemed to be growing.

We endured so many losses. Neighbors, friends, colleagues, teachers, firefighters, exercise instructors—so many people left the Kingdom during this time, as it truly did not reflect the life nor the values they wanted to live. Many moved their families to Bahrain and commuted every day to Arabia. Others protected their assets by sending shipments of their most valuable belongings home to the US for storage and safety. Many employees sent their wives and children home to the US or the UK for a year or two and continued to monitor the situation.

It seemed quite normal and natural to be developing a more fatalistic view of the world. We could never get a bead on the larger picture so why create frustration and fear? I could view the circumstances as grim, or I could choose to focus on the tiny moments in the really good life that we continued to enjoy. Being grateful for a calm day in the face of the danger was the challenge. Hoping for the best and planning an evacuation plan became the norm.

During this time our friendly open-minded schools became a system of fortresses. Ten-foot-high walls and gates staffed with guards round the clock were installed in each school complex. The gates were opened only briefly three times per day to allow school buses inside. Buffer zones with concrete barricades were dragged into place around every facility—schools, recreation areas, the theater and beyond. The office core area, the hub of Aramco, was treated like an airport. Extra guards, stun-guns, X-ray machines and several invisible layers of security were all put in place.

Delta-type barricades that block vehicles from proceeding were built into the roads. Checkpoints were established about half a mile before the gates and manned by Saudi government forces. Jeeps and machine guns were stationed along the route into the compound, transforming this sleepy complex into the high-tech fortress and facility it is now.

ORDERED DEPARTURE

My friend Becky was married to a senior diplomat, Gary Grappo, who had been ambassador in both Oman and Jordan. Up until the early 2000s she accompanied her husband on all foreign assignments. Gary was the Charge D'Affairs or number two at the American Embassy in Riyadh.

After September 11, 2001, political uncertainties on the ground in Arabia together with a satisfying job in the State Department back in DC led Becky to choose to stay in the US. Many wives were to make that decision over the next five years due to the unpredictable spate of threats, bombings and general mischief. A normal life seemed an unreachable dream if one was related to an Embassy staffer in those days.

In 2004 Becky flew to Saudi to visit her family after a reasonable period of orderliness, when there seemed to be a satisfactory lull in terrorist activities. On a Wednesday she hosted a brown bag lunch to talk to US State Department families about their educational concerns, international schools, boarding school and schools in Kingdom in her official role as an education and youth officer for the State Department. Spirits were high, and staff were hoping that things in KSA would settle down and get back to normal. Embassy and Consular staff were thrilled to be reunited with their families and ready to get back to a sense of normalcy once more. All week long there were social events: a party at the embassy, a barbecue at Becky's home and finally the Easter celebration at the ambassador's residence.

The visit was pleasant. Everyone seemed content and happy to be back in the swing of normal life, and by Monday, driving Becky to the airport, Gary enthusiastically sought to persuade Becky to remain in Saudi. By the following Thursday, however, another major terrorist attack incurring deaths and injuries occurred. Gary held a town hall meeting to announce an Ordered Departure—immediate evacuation for all nonessential embassy personnel—on April 15, 2004. This status declares that you are ordered, not invited to leave. The State Department provides support systems to get you to a safe haven, and you may return only when they deem it safe. The result is that families are split up, everyone's lives are interrupted, children are removed from school and inserted into another educational system midyear. Many of these folks were being evacuated for the third time in a short time period. Each time was disrupting, challenging and emotionally exhausting, because you would be leaving loved ones behind in circumstances that were less than predictable.

Just a few days later, on April 19, the US Consulate in Jeddah was attacked by terrorists, and five embassy staff, from Sudan, Yemen, Philippines, India and Sri Lanka, were killed.

Exactly one week after Becky flew home, all nonessential staff from both the embassy in Riyadh and the consulate in Jeddah were ordered to leave, and Becky found herself at Dulles Airport meeting everyone who had attended the picnic, the Easter egg hunt and the barbecue, including her daughter Michelle. While all this was happening, we were in Dhahran reading the newspapers and constant flow of Warden Messages. The *Arab News* reported on compounds that had been attacked and efforts the Saudi government was taking to quell the "deviants," as they called them. We were aware that there were probably influences at work stirring things up, but no details were available.

It would be more than a year before the American Embassy Ordered Departure was finally lifted and American families would be permitted to return to Riyadh, to resume their family lives.

OASIS-TOO CLOSE FOR COMFORT

On May 29, 2004, two attacks happened on oil installations and one on the Oasis, a residential compound in the heart of Al Khobar. The Oasis had a restaurant that we frequented and a skating rink where our friends' kids learned ice hockey. Dozens of expats resided there. Over the course of a day gunmen terrorized the compound, killed twenty-two people and injured many others, including expats from several countries. This finally prompted compound owners to take drastic security measures.

One of our friends assisted the authorities in identifying the terrorists since he had witnessed them scoping out the compound a few days previously. The person whose body was dragged through the streets behind a car was a friend of New Zealand friends of ours, and they were in complete shock. Yet another wave of expats departed the Kingdom.

Saudi security forces found themselves in deadly gun battles with gangs of desperate Al-Qaeda suspects over the next few weeks and months, and the King was calling for all Saudis to report the whereabouts of these "deviants." Weeks of unsteady worry turned into months of chronic low-level concern, which ultimately was diluted down to commonsense observation and living life as normal. Our lifestyle choices were diminished, beach and desert camping— some of the most pleasurable ways to escape the confines of the compound—were restricted, and travel options limited. I sometimes wonder if many of us suffered from a very mild version of anxiety like PTSD during those months.

Once again, more security measures were added. Metal detectors, high-resolution CCTV cameras and other deterrents were eventually put on the entire compound perimeter; meanwhile security guards now drove the perimeter constantly. Security had on its staff a couple of brilliantly qualified individuals who were either ex-MI5, ex-FBI or ex-CIA professionals. One of these characters was overheard announcing that he wished he had had access to similar resources when it was his duty to protect the Queen of England. Several people pointed out to me that every time we entered the compound, we quite innocently drove past enough firepower to stop a small army.

All manner of justifications arose on whether to remain or leave. Increases or changes in security we took as reassuring, and certainly many of us took solace in the idea that Aramco was "too large to fail." The belief was that Aramco, being the largest actor on the global oil stage and supporting the great growing economies of India and China, meant that there was enormous political and economic will-power behind maintaining stability and protecting the infrastructure and ultimately us soft targets. It got to the point that every day free of incidents was a gift.

WHEN THE ABNORMAL BECOMES NORMAL

In January 2005, a mere seven months after the Oasis incident, the Grand Mufti at the Grand Mosque in Mecca announced that extremism should be shunned and non-Muslims were to be welcomed not attacked. This was big news around the Muslim world, as Islamic scholars rarely comment on political issues. He was on television for over three hours to fully explain that Islam is a religion of moderates who choose peace and harmony. I was surprised; this seemed like a shift. Definitely this was designed to be a sea change moment, though only time would tell.

Violence continued. In 2006 there was an attempt to bomb the Aramco facility and scupper an oil field. They came pretty close when a car bomb was detonated between two sets of gates to the facility underneath a large pipe rack. The explosion did minimal damage, but could have caused havoc.

In February 2007, three French nationals were killed and a fourth injured while taking a walk by the roadside near Mada'in Saleh, a Nabotean city in the western region of Saudi. A friend of ours had met these very same people at breakfast that morning in a local restaurant and returned to Dhahran completely shell-shocked by this turn of events.

British, American, Australian and other embassies were constantly advising their citizens to consider whether they needed to travel to the Kingdom due to high threats of terrorist attack. Warden Messages contained mostly vague warnings like "be aware of your surroundings" and "travel in pairs or small groups." After several years of active major and minor incidents the community as a whole viewed these warnings as background noise. These incidents had become irritations that occasionally overshadowed our plans to party in Bahrain or take local trips in and around the Middle East. By the end of 2007 a total of 701 people in Saudi were reported to have had ties to Al-Qaeda or to other terror groups involved or related to planned attacks. We read that many were disposed of by the Government; one wonders what that meant exactly.

Did we feel vulnerable? Yes, sometimes. Were we sitting ducks? That depended on who you asked. There were town hall meetings called to discuss the situation. Many people on the compound had been there during the Gulf War in 1990. They were full of stories, warnings and recollections of how that went.

I observed that many people who had endured the Gulf War seemed to gain prestige and standing within the community by virtue of their war stories. I felt somehow more secure that we were in a community of thrivers, people who had lived through one war and much worse conflict than we were experiencing. Many of this intrepid gang were willing to provide instructions on how to stay calm and soldier on.

BOTTLED UP GRIEF

Neighbors left. The Iraq War started on March 20, 2003, and continued until after we departed the Kingdom. In the face of widespread disruption in the Middle East we watched close friends and people who had become family make shipping arrangements for their stuff, rehome their pets, manage the exit-only process of bureaucracy, make travel reservations and finally distill their belongings down to a few small suitcases. Moving overseas constantly involves painful farewells, for those who depart as well as for those of us who chose to remain behind. My daughter had beloved school friends who left, never to be seen again. A state of low-level grief became the norm.

I think we felt deflated every time we realized there would be another sad departure. We had signed up for this lifestyle, unaware of the emotions these endings would serve up. While the departures were frequently a surprise, one day each of us would move on, and we would leave others behind. How many of these people would we realistically see in the future? How we handled this chaotic field of revolving relationships and navigated the process of goodbyes was frequently influenced by the most recent threat level. The threats were like seesaws—now we are up; oh no, sorry, suddenly we are down.

Some people evaluated the situation on an hourly basis, considering all the options of resigning, splitting up the family or all staying together. I recall John and I having conversations about how to even begin to approach all this stress. How could we even think logically about the action we should or should not be taking? In whom should we place our trust? Did we trust the system, the company or our gut? Some days all three were engaged; other days there was little sign of engagement, and we just plowed forward with our lives. The entire process was a real-life experiment in living life in the face of uncertainty, danger and concern. We learned to pour ourselves into the next semester, the next project, the next horse show. Living in the present and being grateful for the gifts we enjoyed became like a sport, something we had to practice and live up to daily. The idyllic lifestyle bubble had burst, and the messy disruption that arrived in its place was less than welcome.

I lost trust in the system and sometimes faith in government's ability to think clearly. The entire Iraq War changed my perspective on my country of origin, and my new adopted country, the US. This even transformed my political perspectives. Being only several hundred miles from the Iraqi border was too close, in my opinion.

One thing for sure, I felt like the locals continued to be upset and shocked by such violence, the proximity of the war in Iraq and their connection to people who lived there. There was great certainty that no one in Kingdom wanted to bring this furor home. We wondered what the future would contain. Would this be the seeds of some sort of revolution? Reading the *Arab News* and guessing what was happening between the lines was a common pastime. (The *Arab News* is still the most widely read English newspaper of the Eastern

Province.) People were arrested, and many of the terrorists were hunted down and killed. Encouraged by the actions of the government, which seemed to be somewhat successful in stopping several incidents, many of us stayed on.

Every day was filled with roaring jets. Our house was less than a kilometer away from the Dhahran air base. Several sorties per day was the norm. Jets took off overhead and we were mostly in the flight path. They flew in predictable patterns, timings and numbers, many using afterburners. We could see when they were loaded with live bombs. Walking the dog in the evening as jets took off and landed, lighting up a dark sky and roaring furiously overhead, became normal, reasonable and even predictable.

One Monday in 2013, it was early afternoon and I was outside, standing in the dressage ring watching our horse being put through her paces by the instructor. A Tornado belonging to the Saudi Air Force took off and as I glanced overhead I saw the plane literally nose-dive to the ground. Apparently it landed on a small air-base snack bar after encountering technical problems. There was little mention of it in the local news, but it certainly shocked me to see an airplane falling out of the sky. The war was remote, yet it was close in so many ways.

Ultimately all this disruption just folded itself into new shapes, like new origami creations. We each grew in resilience, trust and adaptability. While no one would have chosen this new reality, here it was. It helped to have family discussions, where we would talk it out, express our complaints, worries and fears, then dive right back into the daily tasks that were in front of us, over which we did have some control. We had absolutely zero control over international affairs, only our response to events. Getting creative, taking time away and building delight into every single week became a constant prescription which we dedicated ourselves to wholeheartedly.

مابين اثنين

Part 3
LIMINAL LIVING

The journey is my home.

—Muriel Rukeyser

Chapter 7

THE LAND IN BETWEEN

LAYAKATH COULD STAND SO STILL. A palpable sensation of peace and power emanated from him. A sarong was usually wrapped about around his waist and with rough *keffiyeh* fabric wrapping his ears like a package.

Calm, steady stillness poured out of him in every direction while he simply held Autumn Breeze's halter. He was clearly communicating and managing not only his own energy but that of the 1,800-pound, four-legged beast. Breezy's head was often still, her eyes quiet, almost closed and barely blinking and her curled eyelashes floating like lotus lilies on a pond.

Shifting from hoof to hoof, she would rest her hindquarters and hold strong, waiting for a signal, be it mental or physical, that it was time to move forward. This sleepy pair of statues seemed like one. Several times per week, this was the sight that greeted us at the Dhahran Hobby Farm, where our horse was stabled.

The company horse farm housed about a hundred horses and was staffed by a team of Indian, Nepalese, Bangladeshi and Filipino fellows who lived, ate, slept and worked with this herd of gorgeous animals. The horses were owned by both native Saudis and expats. Owning and caring for a horse in Arabia was one of our exercises in liminal living.

For our daughter's eleventh birthday in 2003 we purchased a beautiful mare called Wilma from a stable in Bahrain, where she had arrived from Australia. Lynsey promptly named her Autumn Breeze. Owning an Australian quarter horse in Arabia seemed like a dream come true. I had never owned horses before; however, I had learned to ride as a child and enjoyed spending time around them. The horses were a calm, stable influence during somewhat turbulent times in Arabia. They lived in the present and required us to be right there with them.

Although we arrived in Arabia with ideas of what we might achieve as a result of parking ourselves in the camel lane, we had never discussed owning a horse. The addition was a spontaneous decision that brought added responsibilities, an entrée into an entirely different world—the world of "horsey people"—and great joy in seeing our daughter grow up with plenty of fun. Owning our horse was a gift that changed our daily routines and expanded our circles. We were constantly interacting and working closely with the grooms who managed the care, feeding, walking and well-being of our animal.

Our groom Layakath was Nepalese. His family lived close to the

Indian-Nepal border. A devout Muslim, he was quiet, steady and one of the most substantial human beings I have ever met. Watching him attending to the duties of caring for the five horses he was responsible for was like observing effortless elegance in action. He seemed to juggle his responsibilities and life with quintessential Eastern ease. To me he seemed to be chopping wood and carrying water, as the Buddhists recommend.

I arrived in Arabia as one person, but I certainly departed as another. The care and keeping of our horse was just one cross-cultural adventure in partnering with others who were different, neither more nor less, right or wrong, just different. I feel like I was changed at depth by the day-to-day interaction with Layakath.

The Oxford dictionary describes a paradigm as a worldview, usually subconscious, that affects all of our thinking. Whether I knew it or not, my paradigms were always working and always on display to the world in the form of my imagination, memories, perceptions and intuition. Being grateful for the accident of birth in Scotland as a female instead of in Nepal as a male was one of them. I had not necessarily earned my comfortable life, but I could surely learn from observing Layakath's life and the sacrifice of living away from his wife and children for so many years.

The new paradigms sometimes created positive and healthy disruption. The new potency of my feeling of gratitude was a paradigm that changed for me over the course of my time in Arabia. I was suddenly grateful for this new community, called the Hobby Farm, although it was a bumpy ride in terms of belonging to a community that I frequently didn't understand. I recall getting yelled at by one instructor for taking another instructor's advice in managing a horsey situation. Passion overflowed in the horsey community, frequently a mysterious force to me. I managed to reframe these intense reactions and chalked them up to fierce devotion to life in general and horses in particular.

Although my life layover in Arabia effectively changed some parts of me, it was not the end of dealing with paradigms. It seems like life consists of the creation, navigation and termination of paradigms that lead us to the next level of existence. Throughout our daily lives in Arabia we could be living normally and naturally, as if we were in the West, until suddenly we were confronted with a multicultural moment that reminded me that, indeed, we were building daily skills in the middle zones.

BROTHERS, BIRDING AND BEAUTY

Rugged traditional carpets were thrown across the sand like large leaves. We sat facing the line where heaven and earth seemed to meet while the setting sun floated downward like a giant hazy balloon. As it sank closer and closer to the horizon, I was entertained by the live and deeply personal falconry show going on around me.

Sitting on the sand, watching the huge red sun dip below the horizon, I heard but two sounds. One was a distant bell attached to a camel heading for the makeshift wooden fence and compound he called home. The other was the *whoop, whoop* of the lure line with a treat on it that was being circled by the Saudi falconers, with a falcon swooping past the lure at over fifty miles per hour. Falconry training in the desert: a mystical pursuit with one of nature's fiercest and fastest creatures. Bliss.

Right there, right then, I felt like I was suspended somehow between two worlds. The bright new technical twenty-first century was clearly in evidence. Our falconry hosts had driven up in the most up-to-date and beautiful Land Cruisers, fully equipped with sophisticated tech and telemetry systems for tracking the birds. These birds were valued at several thousand dollars: one does not want to take a chance that they might just fly away. Drinking Arabic coffee, eating dates, cross-legged on those hairy carpets, I found even breathing seemed to still, like life was happening in slow motion. I was struck by that feeling of weightlessness and timelessness, as though we could choose in that moment to leap backward to Mohammed's time 1,500 years ago or forward to a distant and as-yet undefined future.

Very occasionally we landed into an activity that embraced and even sought to bridge the two centuries we were living in. One of those experiences was a magical ten days in November 2008 during my brother-in-law Rob's visit to the Kingdom.

Rob Palmer is a world-renowned falcon photographer, and his visit revealed a window into the curious world of Arabic tradition and culture we were not even aware of. Rob was on a worldwide photography tour, taking photographs for *Sky Hunters*, a coffee table book on birds of prey. Prior to his arrival in Kingdom, he had visited Spain, Oman, Dubai and Abu Dhabi to meet falconers and study their methods and traditions, including the birds' feeding, training and flying exercises, which varied across the globe.

When Rob asked to visit us, he also asked if we could arrange to meet some Saudi falconers. John's assistant, Mayessa, contacted two interested cousins to make the connections.

John, Rob and I sat on rough mats, surrounded by three Saudi professionals and seven hawks resting quietly on their sturdy perches secured in the sand. I was surprised by the air of affection and honor the falconers extended the birds. After its hood was removed, each bird would be released for training using a lure, a small piece of meat attached to a leather cord. The birds would dip, dive and maneuver at top speed to catch the lure, while the falconer's job was to assure that the lure was just out of their reach. After the training, the Saudis would carefully take their falcon onto their glove and feed them treats with the greatest affection.

Falconry records in Arabia date to the seventeenth century BC, and the Arab world has one of the largest communities of falconers anywhere. Falconry is a mixture of sport, social tradition and cultural significance. Many falconers are trained at a young age to handle the birds, and they grow up in families who camp, fly their birds and spend the remainder of the day reciting their stories. Falconry requires patience, flexibility and a deep sense of relationship between the bird and man, with a strong dose of modern-day technology thrown in.

One of the common denominators of the Saudi falconers we met was their excitement to share their sport and make us welcome. For many Saudis it is an all-consuming lifestyle or an idyllic respite from busy Western workplace stress. Many executives working at high-level positions in corporations can be found out in the desert in the evenings and on weekends, far away from the madding crowds, communing with nature and flying their birds. Sadly, it is a masculine sport, and women do not tend to take an interest. However, there are plenty of female veterinarians and other professionals who support the sport.

Saudi falconers are proud to personally demonstrate the dignity of their birds and the deep-seated traditions going back hundreds of years. They are normally willing to interact with expats to share their passion. Deirdre remembered an incident when her family was celebrating a Thanksgiving feast in the desert, dozens of miles from the compound. A small white Toyota pickup, commonly used for transporting camels, came bouncing over the horizon and joined the assemblage of vehicles around their encampment. Three energetic young Saudi men sprang from the truck and proceeded to practice their English on the group while they offered a couple of falcons for inspection. They let the kids put on the falconer's glove and hold the falcons. Their willingness to share their novel gift was delightful. As an extra surprise, they returned the next day with the quintessential camel for the boys to ride.

THE BIRD HOTEL

Another gem of an experience occurred when Rob, John and I visited the falconry store in Dammam. Finding the store even with Saudi guides proved challenging in the dark evening, as we plunged down lanes and raced across parking lots, careening around the oldest and oddest parts of Dammam. Mayessa came along for the ride but chose to wait in the car. I imagine few Westerners had visited this area, and certainly the shop owners were unused to having a Western woman in the building. Tolerant and modestly welcoming as usual, they acknowledged my presence only with the slight lowering of their eyelashes. Rob and Mayessa's cousins proceeded to have long conversations with the shopkeeper on the technology surrounding falconry. Rob naturally assumed the role of professor and technical translator for us. The shop was packed full to the rafters with falconry gear: hoods, gloves and lures; telemetry receivers, tracking devices and high-tech transmitters. The reliance of the sport on a mixture of extremely high- and low-tech equipment was fascinating. My gift, or *baksheesh*, that night was a tiny handmade leather hood, beautifully hand-stitched, which I treasure even now.

After visiting the store, we were driven to a dark, spooky compound; there were no street lamps, and it felt like a scene from a B movie. Our female guide again declined to accompany us into the compound; however, as usual, the Saudi fellows encouraged me to participate. I felt some reluctance, but armed in the ubiquitous *abaya* and head scarf, I took a deep breath and stepped over the threshold. I was instantly entranced by another world. Initially it seemed dark and somewhat disorganized and dingy. It took a while for my eyes to adjust to the dimly lit shadowy areas. Inside there were a couple of nondescript makeshift buildings with open-air *majlis* dotted with low, upholstered sofas in traditional Saudi fabric, well-worn and lumpy looking. Five large and heavily bearded Saudi men lounged around smoking a *hookah*, their mumblings muted yet constant.

Our host, leading the way, had prepared them in Arabic for a visit from several Westerners. There was much *Alhamdil-allah*-ing and preliminary explanations as to the reason for our visit and who exactly Rob and John were. I, of course, was just there as a witness, or an afterthought.

I assumed this was the equivalent of a pub in Scotland or Ireland, a "third place" where these people met and discussed their passion for falconry. I sensed a subconscious reaction to my presence, but as with so many of my interactions with Saudis, not a single bit of body language was evident. They barely glanced, darkly, at me, then continued their conversation, smoking the hookah pipes by their sides. I was to be tolerated not welcomed—at least, not yet. They were not going to challenge my presence into what felt like an inner sanctum. We moved to an adjacent building where approximately thirty hooded, molting birds were tethered to perches in the middle of an enormous sandbox. The birds had been tethered there for approximately four months during the summer while their feathers grew back in preparation for the upcoming flying season. Most evenings, their owners would check on the birds, tell war stories about their conquests and catch up with local falconry gossip.

After some halting discussion involving translation by one of Mayessa's cousins, everyone relaxed and started to become curious and ask questions. Rob's expertise on falcons, including names, details and stories carried us through the encounter comfortably. Ultimately one of the bird owners warmed up enough to invite me to hold one of the falcons using a glove. The birds are highly intelligent; you can almost feel them sending out signals using all their senses. Holding the falcon was easy; being in such close proximity to Saudi men on their native turf was surprisingly unnerving and disquieting for me. I felt like an ugly interloper who had barged in on some sacred male ritual. This was one of very few moments that I can recall feeling deeply foreign and alien. I had lived in the Kingdom for fourteen years at this point, yet in a sense the country was growing and becoming an even bigger mystery. What other hidden depths would be revealed to me before I departed?

TEENAGERS ARE TEENAGERS THE WORLD OVER

In the middle of a bleak, barren and uncompromisingly boring desert in Bahrain stands the Tree of Life, a 500-year-old acacia tree that issues its sprawling branches from the desert with a fierce determination. As the sun set the day we were there, the sky became hazier, a deep fuzzy gray with a giant orange sun in the background. Rob, John and I met a local man there, who told us there were several Bahraini teenagers flying their falcons nearby. We changed direction and quickly pulled up to a ragtag group of all shapes and sizes. Most of them were proudly clutching their falcons and prattling away. After we greeted them, Rob waded into their midst and quickly became the established expert. With no Arabic at all, Rob helped them identify their falcons; they laughed and asked questions in Arabish for a while. It was fascinating to watch a common passion become the bridge for a boisterous conversation and cross-cultural meeting. This was a terrific conclusion to a great week of immersion and exposure to the mystery of falconry and its significance in Arabia. We loved Rob's visit; it made the place more real. Time spent with falconers of all ages had opened our eyes to reveal one of the great wonders of this magnificent country, so carefully hidden in plain sight. Being exposed to the raw nature of ancient Saudi was a tonic to the expat malaise that constantly threatened to descend.

We were treated to several copies of *Sky Hunters* the following year. Half of the book's photos were taken by Rob. About ten of them were taken during his time with us.

GROWING UP BETWEEN CULTURES

Many children in the community were actually born in the Kingdom, several of them are second- and third-generation Aramcons.

Aramco advertises that the biggest perk of moving to Arabia was family life—this was true. A frequently shared comparison is made to life in the 1950s and 1960s, similar to *Leave It to Beaver*: a place where families played together, children attended school together and parents worked alongside each other, then coached their children in baseball, soccer or swimming in the evenings. Both children and dads usually ate lunch at home. Neighbors and friends became like extended family. There was a keen sense that the village or community was raising the children together.

Children ran wild through the compound—down the beaches, over the *jebels* (small rocky hills) and around the Hobby Farm perimeter.

Our kids grew up with a sense of freedom that was sustained by boundaries in the form of a perimeter, security gates and wire fences. There was an unwritten rule that the entire compound community looked out for the children. They could bicycle to the Hobby Farm and ride their horses—sometimes out of the farm and into the subdivision. I will never forget meeting a mum in the Commissary who reported she had had a visit from eleven-year-old Lynsey and her pal Jacqueline. This gal was remarkably sanguine about the fact that both girls were on horseback and the horses were casually standing on her front lawn munching on the sweet grass. Thankfully, she chose to see the humorous side of this escapade and was extremely gracious about hoof prints left behind on her lawn. To this day, children can explore relatively freely within the safe boundaries of the compound.

Whether earning Girl Scout badges, dancing with Miss Sandra's ballet and jazz dance troupes, swimming on the swim team or hanging out at the recreation center, movie theater or bowling alley, after 9/11 the children all required a form of identification to gain access. Each family had a badge number, which became emblazoned on the hearts and minds of generations of young people. Ask any Aramcon; no matter whether they lived there in the 1950s or three years ago, they will remember their badge number.

Although definite cultural divides existed between the local and expat populations, many positive alliances formed; for example, expat and Saudi girls alike played and learned together in the same Girl Scout troops. Girl Scouts has had a long thriving history of teaching skills and exploration in the Kingdom. Boy Scouts also had an enormous presence. These types of interactions among families lent themselves to developing empathy and smoothing the obvious boundaries of radical social differences, ultimately harmonizing them to produce a society that was unique in all the world. To this day many Aramco kids who grew up together on the compound remain closely connected.

The security guards were for the most part warm, welcoming and charming with our kids. One year our daughter's birthday party consisted of a treasure hunt. The local firehouse was one of the stops on the hunt. The Saudi fellows loved having the children clamber over the fire truck and were marvelous hosts.

Walking down one of the hallways at Dhahran Middle School, within a few steps you would hear Spanish, Arabic, French and, of course, English. The sensation of a multilingual community all working, studying and living in harmony had a magical quality I still long for: that sense of the entire world united and working together in a harmonious and common purpose. While this sounds idyllic and altruistic, were there moments where cultural intelligence was lacking, respect missing and friction emerging between differing lifestyles? Oh yes, but when they did arise, for the most part all kids, parents and faculty learned to accentuate the positives, focus on the shared interests and take a deep breath and practice some mindfulness. The constant practice of returning to those values kept the entire system on track. Somehow the multicultural community articulated a high value on raising well-adapted, highly educated global citizens designed to perpetuate a multicultural world that works for all. From the hiring and training of teachers to curriculum and school policy development, a high intention was placed on turning out kids who would consider themselves global citizens. The kids themselves naturally developed an intention to make the world function better. Diversity and inclusion were baked into the entire experience.

THE THIRD CULTURE

We were privileged to take long and exotic trips to different continents, where we made an effort to expose Lynsey to differing peoples, cultures and languages. One of the older Aramco kids, Natasha Burge, wrote, "[P]eople are people everywhere you go, more alike than different in all the ways that count." What a valuable lesson to learn for global citizens.

Elizabeth recounts that one year during their annual vacation back to the US, they placed their third grader in a summer camp.

After school the teacher approached Elizabeth and wondered why her daughter would make up so many stories of riding elephants in Thailand, going on safari and swimming with dolphins in the Arabian Sea, and Elizabeth had to explain that these were no fantasies but actual real life she had experienced. There is no education system in the world that can teach children quite like the classroom called "international travel."

Most of the kids associated "home" with where the parents and kids were residing. Disassociated from their parents' cultures, our kids grew up in a company culture, the Saudi culture and then a greater expatriate culture. They learned to juggle realities, hidden boundaries and invisible cultural divides. A little blond-haired girl from Texas was asked by her teacher where home was; "Saudi Arabia" was the answer.

Families from countries like Pakistan, India, Lebanon and Egypt managed to instill and adopt some of their home culture and values in the face of Western programming. Since the education system was based on the US system, and the majority of kids were from the US, Canada and the UK, the prevailing culture was Western. However, frequently I would hear a kid say, "But that is not my family culture," and then go on to explain how their family approached such and such.

While children were aware of the invisible cultural lines, for the most part they navigated them well. At school, they functioned in the multicultural soup, then behind closed doors back home they might switch to their parents' native language, ethnic cooking and religious practices. Behind the front doors of those neat Western subdivision-like rows, families spoke different languages and ate dramatically different foods, and practiced a variety of faiths.

Naturally, cultural dissonance emerged and small conflicts arose, but for the most part we would just say to ourselves something like "Ah yes, that's how they would think about it in such-and-such's family," because they were Lebanese or Egyptian or Syrian. Surfing the waves of interculturalism became natural, easy and almost second nature. We lived with the assumption that this was life, and we were blessed, grateful and happy to live in this constant kaleidoscope of culture and diversity. We built elastic mindsets that stretched to include each other's diversity.

I met Ruth van Reken through Families in Global Transition, a forum for globally mobile families and those who work with them. This organization and her book *Third Culture Kids* were very instructive in processing life overseas. My educational research also made me aware of the cultural gap between my own upbringing and the way we were raising Lynsey.

Third or cross culture kids live, grow and are fashioned by the liminal lifestyle of expatriates. Although I spent my formative years in Scotland, I set off overseas in my early twenties while my brain was still being developed. I married a second generation TCK.

Aramco kids came from all different backgrounds. Dhahran was blessed with several families from different parts of Africa. One African family had three gorgeous children called Gift, Precious and ThanksGod. When the time came to apply for boarding school, they had to write an essay about their life. Gift arrived at the counselor's office and asked her what she should write. Diane, being a seasoned school counselor, never answered the question but returned a question: "What was the most interesting thing about moving to Aramco?"

Gift responded, "Well, we live in a palace."

Her family was living in an average Aramco employee home. Most of us considered the houses nothing special at best. In fact in many ways they were way below the standards expected by Americans. But Gift remembered living in a mud hut in Africa when she was younger. Their dad attended school and became educated, and the family saved constantly. Eventually their dad was rewarded by getting this amazing Aramco job, which meant they could live in what she now considered a palace. What a great perspective.

Diane participated as a chaperone of the service projects that took the kids to Zululand in South Africa. The kids worked hard to raise funds. They took school supplies and money to the same school for over a decade. Toward the end of one of those trips the kids got the opportunity to bathe the AIDS babies. The act of tenderly handling these precious beings was a moment seared into the hearts and minds of the students and chaperones for a lifetime. When Lynsey took the school trip to Zululand, her teacher/chaperone would send little notes every few days to catch the parents up on how the kids were doing. He shared their itinerary, which was often a mixture of fun outdoor and natural history-like activities such as quad-biking, hiking and indoor climbing. The highlight of these trips was taking hard-earned fundraising funds to the same school and actually giving it to the school. One day we received a note indicating how the students including Lynsey seemed to be changed at depth by simply observing and interacting with the children who wore perfectly turned out uniforms and walked often up to ten miles each way to attend school.

During another service trip to Africa, Diane and a colleague were responsible for all the Arabic kids, while another two teachers were working closely with the Caucasian kids. One night one of the Arabic kids said, "So explain why we are all together on your team?"

Diane responded, "Didn't you guys choose each other as roommates?" They nodded. "And did you write your first and second choice as roommates?" They conceded they had. She followed this up with, "You in fact chose each other and your own crew." They had been about to get uppity about the intercultural divide when in fact they had self-selected into tribes of their own choosing. She then told them, "But you know what—I chose you," and that, of course, made them feel better. Self-selection of friends across cultures was always a bonus.

GROWING TOWARD GLOBAL-HEARTEDNESS

On one occasion an eighth grader reported to a teacher she was going to be married off when she turned eighteen years old. When asked how she felt about that, she responded that she hated it. A few days later she reported that she had given the matter some consideration, and had told her family she would accept being married but it could not happen until she had completed her education and degree. She later reported to her teacher, "You should be proud of me."

Another kid had written a poem about the situation in his homeland, Lebanon. He talked about how he had considered the violence and fighting to be "cool" but had revised his position and now understood how dreadfully sad it was. When he got up to read his poem, he said, "I saw my friend from Sudan, another girl from Pakistan and my friend from India sitting there," and he thought,

They too have been through this. Each of their home countries had suffered from division, war, disruption and dissonance. On the spot he changed the lines in the poem from "me" to "we" and from "my village" to "our village." He reflected on the shared experiences of pain at a deeper level. The ultimate lesson in being global-hearted citizens is in building bridges with empathy. Aramco kids learned this at a very young age.

A new seventh grader arrived fresh from Texas. He shared that his dad had experienced some trouble and this job with Aramco was, "saving our bacon." He then overheard another student saying, "I can't believe my parents are making me go with them to London again. Does this make me sound like a brat?" while rolling her eyes with a great shaking of hair. The new student burst out, "You get to go to London—and again, like you have been before? That sounds mighty exciting to me." He was immediately beyond thrilled that he might actually get to go sometime in the future himself. Opportunities to expand and grow emotionally, physically and socially were built into the lifestyle every day at school.

Frequently members of the same family were born in different countries; therefore, kids looked beyond divisive labels—they were required to in order to function within the social, school and compound system.

GROWING UP WITH WAR

During the Gulf War, the kids carried gas masks to school and hid beneath their desks when air raid sirens wailed overhead. One of their favorite things to score were MREs (Meals Ready to Eat) left by the military, and they loved finding military leftovers and camo-anything.

Scud missiles were used during this war. Being less than reliable, they frequently disintegrated in midair or were shot down by Patriot missiles, sometimes landing in pieces on the compound. Older kids enjoyed searching and finding remains from the war; they were considered terrific souvenirs. Lynsey had a classmate called Scud, and a certain group of kids considered themselves the Scud Kids, as author Natasha Burge remembers.

Irene recalls growing up in Ras Tanura in the 1960s. Scraping tar off her feet after walking on the beach was normal. She remembers people boarding buses in front of the school getting ready to evacuate the compound during 1967 due to the Six-Day War and some rioting by the locals. Women would cry then wave goodbye—Irene's family stayed behind.

She also recalls the fighter planes flying just over the house and the vibrations they caused during the war. There seems to be a pattern here, because she and I have similar memories but four decades apart.

Kids are intuitive and curious. The combination of the two traits gives them the impetus to navigate these invisible lanes naturally. They grew skills to argue in favor of any side of an argument, which gives them a leg up on monocultural kids. They can hold several opposing ideas simultaneously.

Big hidden subjects live within the liminal living gap. Subjects like unresolved grief, cultural sensitivity and an expanded worldview are all products of this space. For many of us mums, we sent our children to boarding schools in other countries, many in Europe, Canada and the USA. One day we were a mum visiting our children in a Western culture, and the next day we would be flying home to the Eastern Province and assuming differing professional and social roles. Within the space of twenty-four hours we would be required to juggle food, language, environment and time changes. Frequently it felt like a real live quantum leap through time and space. Ultimately we landed into an environment with beliefs and practices handed down over four centuries. Suffice it to say that decades' worth of Western women became absolute masters at handling massive amounts of change.

While we observed the local culture, we had to keep in mind that the stereotypes did not necessarily apply to individuals we met. We enjoyed interactions with Saudis and had several Saudi families as neighbors, but we also learned where the intercultural lines lay. We felt completely at ease in Saudi, Bahrain and the US—wherever you found us—but simultaneously belonged wholeheartedly to none of those places.

Living in between meant living in between the wealthiest and the poorest. As levels of security fluctuated, our mindsets would shift depending on international events and circumstances, and we discovered new coping skills. We understood that our values might be different from others, but as people, we were interested in the same things. Willing to give up a few Western cultural ideas and adopt the Saudi calendar with its generous holiday system, oh yes, but we also imported our traditions and shared many of them openly. We could pick and choose what celebrations, foods, even languages we wanted to experiment with. Each of us was pretty much enrolled as a citizen diplomat, hopefully, offering a positive perspective on the West during that period of time.

Chapter 8

EAST MEETS WEST—WHICH WAY IS BEST?

SENDING OUR ONLY DAUGHTER to boarding school was the most painful part of my journey as a mum in Saudi.

I remember the surroundings more than the conversation: an Italian coffee shop with bistro-style woven rattan chairs, round tables with glass circles and rattan window coverings. This conversation was about the offer my parents had just made to send me to a Christian boarding school in Wales that had horse riding. They were really seeking to give me, their beloved only and adopted daughter, the best possible education. I was neither impressed by Wales nor the by fact that it was a "Christian" boarding school (I had visions of being locked up). Apparently, I rolled my eyes and told my mother that I would prefer to stay in our wee hometown of 10,000 people and take my chances. In hindsight I wish I had taken the leap.

I never imagined that four decades later I would be faced with a similar conversation with my one and only daughter. It was almost like history repeating itself.

MY ONE AND ONLY THIRD CULTURE KID

Lynsey was born in California. I never doubted for one moment that she would grow up as a global soul. Ultimately her outlook was a product of her parents' international backgrounds multiplied by the Aramco school system. Impressionable and open, she naturally absorbed the interests and attitudes of a global citizen in the Aramco bubble. Her Scottish mother's perspective seemed to carry little influence; however, the collective community and school system provided a wonderful structure within which children could discover themselves.

Journeying to the US almost every single year on vacation (called "repat") over the years, I saw that I was never going to influence her to self-identify with Scotland or the UK. We would visit the UK, hug Grandma and Grandpa, walk the dog, play a few games, and then she was ready and open for the next adventure; that was as much Scottish culture as she could feign an interest in. Although she and I have British passports and I carried the programming of British culture, she never would, unless she moved there. Was I raising a kid who would find herself feeling like an alien? I had found the US to be the most difficult culture to adopt—how could I teach her to be something I had never really been? What subtle messages was I passing along to her?

I wanted her to grow up to be the best, most generous and positive person she could be. Beyond those parameters I was unattached as to whether she would choose to become British or American or something else. As part of a floating tribe of expats or global nomads, I was entirely peaceful with this conclusion and hopeful that my daughter would adopt that perception yet build her own roots. Expats or global nomads are now a tribe of 258 million, according to the United Nations; soon there will be more multiculturals on the globe than American nationals.

Shortly after Lynsey's big move up to the Dhahran Middle School, the Aramco sixth-grade teachers introduced the concept of boarding school. Aramco decided many years ago that educating, entertaining and monitoring children in Kingdom from tenth grade onward was not in their wheelhouse. The sixth-grade classes were housed under the same roof as kids about to leave in one, two or three years. The concept became infectious. Lynsey's classmates had older siblings who were already attending boarding school or were about to leave for that next adventure.

We were certainly not keen to send away our one and only; on the other hand we were extremely keen to take advantage of all the possibilities of living overseas and of the great education opportunities that were available. We began actively imagining the situation with Lynsey. By seventh grade what once was a mere balloon of possibility sitting on the horizon began to feel like a meteorite hurtling toward us, one we needed to jump on and ride all the way.

We were advised by the school counselors to start early, stay focused, visit schools and ask as many questions as possible. Applications were prepared at the commencement of ninth grade, so in grades seven and eight we needed to get busy. Because of the distance, time and energy that went into every trip back to the US, we began to feel the pressure and the need to plan. This included listing all the boarding schools that we would visit, the times, order and their suitability. Lynsey drew up her rubric of what she was looking for in a school community—the facilities available, the sports and hobbies offered, and even the geography and weather were factors in this amazingly complex document she created.

We attended presentations from ten boarding school representatives who came to Dhahran to highlight their school's education program, boarders' lifestyles, activities and curriculum. We considered location, flying time, culture, educational results and small or large school size. Lynsey's interests were the primary driving force, so we considered the arts, sports and locations that were at the top of her list.

By eighth grade the kids were being offered practice standardized high school tests to hone their skills. We visited schools in the US, the UK, Canada and Switzerland. Secretly I was wishing that Lynsey would choose a school in the UK or Switzerland, and thus have what I considered the benefit of a European education on top of her Dhahran-American education. However, this was not to be, as she rejected the European choices.

I wondered exactly how we could expect a fourteen- or fifteen-year-old to make such a momentous decision. Because most of the kids in the class were headed the same direction, it was easier to go with the flow, which meant sharing notes and comparing stories with other families. We felt we were not alone, and this helped us justify what I would have considered a draconian choice.

Lynsey interviewed very well. Eventually, she was accepted to the four schools she applied to in the US and Canada. After some advising conversations with her half-sister, Lynsey chose a school in Colorado. Number one, she was not keen on uniforms and both Canadian schools had uniforms; two, she was still keen on riding, and Fountain Valley offered riding; and three, she would be close to family with her sister and grandparents in Denver. Finally, the Colorado school climbed to the top of the pile in terms of her desires and being a good fit with the type of people she met there. For the most part she could recognize and imagine herself into that environment. Fountain Valley was a great choice for her, with enough diversity, plenty of European and Asian students and several Aramco kids. She was content.

During Aramco spring break in her ninth grade, acceptance letters were sent to prospective students, with Lynsey receiving one from Fountain Valley. Another layer of reality settled in like a fog bank. Clearly, I had built my idea of motherhood out of proportion. One of my two primary roles for a decade and a half was about to transform itself upon her departure. The sense of a gaping hole opening up in my life's pathway was ominous. To me, the boarding school application process felt like a runaway train, and we were somehow hanging onto the roof, the way people in India ride on trains.

I was a walking puzzle of complex feelings; however, I was also part of a small army of women all marching in step and sending our kids off to boarding school. This was almost a rite of passage for the mums, let alone the kids. The army provided structure and comfort.

Finally, the moment arrived when Lynsey and I were in the hallway, packed suitcases at our feet, light from the left, light from the right shining through the living room as we stood heart to heart. Lynsey, already taller by five inches than I, looked around her, down at me, and I quietly told her that now was her moment to choose. I invited her to speak any qualms, doubts or wobblies and said it was perfectly OK to change her mind.

Her big eyes, brown like walnuts, looked back bravely. She nodded, gave me a perfunctory hug and walked without hesitation toward the door. She was on her way.

That's my girl, I thought to myself, much braver than I and learning to "do it afraid" at such an early age.

There are women who have raised several children in these circumstances and who have successfully sustained that lifestyle for one or two decades or more. I have so much empathy, appreciation and respect for the toughness, logistics and focus it took to manage children living away at boarding school for so many years. I also have to give a shout-out to the tenacity, grace and resilience these women demonstrated when faced with the inevitable challenges that come along with teenagers who are suddenly enjoying more freedom and facing educational challenge and displacement all at the same time. I knew of multiple families where either the mother ended up moving back to the US near the student's school or the child returned to Saudi to go to the local high school at the Dhahran consulate. This journey was clearly not for everyone.

FAR, FAR AWAY—HEARTS WALKING AROUND ON TWO CONTINENTS

During the first year of my daughter's boarding school career, I remained in the US from August when we dropped her off at school with great fanfare and excitement until October when parents' weekend rolled around. Living in the US for a few months was an exercise in using my brain differently. It had been thirteen years since I had last lived there, and the change factor was overwhelming. Nevertheless, I did the best I could to get my head around the US system. Complex problems and questions that challenged my new value system kept cropping up in front of me, and I wasn't sure how to manage it all.

My friend Karyl to this day reminds me of my meltdown in the milk aisle, the day an ordinary trip to the grocery store turned into a complex cultural episode. I had dropped my groceries in the checkout line and ran back to pick up milk—but there weren't only one or two choices of milk, as I was accustomed to in the Commissary in Dhahran; there were about twenty choices. Various colors, descriptions and percentages were visible. Choices unimagined, uninvited and unwanted loomed large on the shelf, pushing my brain into overwhelm. I was hit by a sense of panic. I would just refuse to choose. Yes, leave the store without the milk. "Who needs it anyway?" would become my mantra. Almost everyone who has lived abroad has at one point had a parallel experience.

Upon returning to the US full time three years later, I was to become very familiar with this reaction. I needed to learn to interrupt the pattern of overwhelm and judgment that threatened to swamp me. The oversupply of goods, services and choices back "home" became a conundrum that had me questioning my values. To this day, I tend to seek simplicity, to streamline, to look for clean lines, to shy away from purchasing duplicates or bundles as we did in Arabia. I watch myself get easily overwhelmed by the overabundance of choices that don't add to my quality to life. My muddled brain enjoys and seeks out white space and simplicity. I believe this is partly due to having lived the liminal life jumping back and forth between cultures and having to keep so many cultural details straight.

Arriving back in Dhahran after dropping Lynsey at boarding school, our home seemed like a quiet and lonely nest, too peaceful, too quiet. Every trip past her bedroom, gazing at the all-too-unnaturally tidy blue, cream and tan bedspread with the big paisley border—left exactly as if she had gone to school—yelled loss like a siren. Lynsey's absence felt almost like a death. Indeed, it was an ending to the sweet everyday family life we had enjoyed for fifteen years. I grieved; each of us with kids at school found ways to grieve ourselves through the process.

We developed a family year-long calendar with a clear timeline that showed school terms, our visits and the parents' weekends. Calendaring time together, planning and building toward visits became a framework for our lives. There were days when I missed her presence so much that I ached. I started to question my purpose. I was no longer a hands-on mum, and we were heading toward our last years in Kingdom—then what? I needed to settle myself and my mind down in order to cope. While everyone in Arabia understood the almighty boarding school dilemma, it seemed that no one in the US did. When we talked to family and friends back home, they were puzzled by our choice. In fact, most people's response was, "Oh dear, what did she do? Is she in rehab?" or words to that effect. Boarding school was another way our exceptional experiences divided us from our US-based friends instead of bonding us. Suddenly we fell into a "privileged" category because we were enjoying a huge benefit that most families couldn't even begin to imagine. This alone required delicate conversations and handling among family members.

Meantime we talked to Lynsey whenever we could. We had purchased Dolce & Gabbana gold flip phones prior to leaving her at school and were delighted with the technology—we could speak to her regularly. By Christmas when she returned on her own, traveling from Colorado to Saudi Arabia, we knew she was well on her way. She handled the travel brilliantly even when her itinerary got changed and she was diverted to various cities.

Since kindergarten Lynsey's friends at the Aramco school were Swiss, French, Dutch, American, Canadian, Egyptian, Jordanian, Pakistani, Indian and others. Barely aware of nationality and naturally embracing diversity, she just knew that the kids in her class had names like Ahmed, Anwar, Mo for Mohammad and other non-Anglo-Saxon names. We watched her move out into the world at boarding school with a calmness and solid acceptance for her new situation, faculty and classmates. A global heart was beating out in the world, and we were curious about where this would all lead.

BACK AT THE COMPOUND

For the next three years I wondered if I would need at some point to forgive myself for sending her away to boarding school. Would she feel like she had been sent away, and would she forgive us for making this choice? I found that changing my thinking in small increments helped immensely to calm my mind and stay upbeat. We had minimal distractions, we stuck to the schedule and managed to see each other almost every ten to twelve weeks. Was it always easy—no; was it possible—yes!

Determined to fill my life with positive habits that would calm my mind and be a steadying influence, I tackled Tai Chi. I started taking lessons with my friend Lisa, who had been studying for a couple of years. We met on Sunday and Tuesday mornings at the recreation center, which had a large gymnasium with wood floors and mirrors. Tai Chi became a beautiful practice that helped center and ground me. Occasionally we would practice as a demonstration team, all wearing colorful, traditional Chinese outfits. As a group, about seven of us went on to learn the fan style, and I also participated in some preliminary sword events. I enjoyed the artistic expression, the personal focus it helped build and the calming effect on my mindset.

In hindsight, I now understand I was rewiring myself and my body by practicing this calming discipline. Neuroscience now reveals that practicing a physical discipline like Tai Chi can help us to process loss. I witnessed myself becoming calmer, more centered, and I believe my brain was adapting to my new reality. Frequently grief would gain the upper hand, but with steady practice and dedication, it took a back seat. The entire three years spent practicing Tai Chi were a time of amazing productivity and joy, even in the face of an empty house, dinners for two and multiple trips across oceans to see each other.

How do we feel today? I hope we are all reconciled to the decision, and Lynsey attributed the journey to making her next transition to college so much easier and more effective. Although I wish I had enjoyed the sweet presence of my daughter for those three years, I do not for a moment regret the decision when I consider the person she grew up to be and the wonderful opportunities that boarding school presented. Privileged we were, and grateful.

Having the support of a community, many of whom had a history and practice of sending their kids away, helped tremendously. We also had a three-month-long visit from my elderly dad during our final year in Arabia, which kept us entertained and engaged.

STRONG WINGS, SHALLOW ROOTS

Now a grown woman working in the US, Lynsey has adopted Ireland as her third nationality, due to her grandmother's birth there. Her collage of memories is built upon having strong wings and shallow roots, and we watch her and her friends balancing the impulse to travel and soar with the deep desire for a supportive community. While everything about our community was designed to mentor and grow self-sufficient global citizens, it also was an organizing principle in which these kids lived. Birth, health, social life, recreation, school then boarding school were completely taken care of by the Aramco system.

Nan's daughter Hannah went to China on a study-abroad program and plans on becoming totally fluent in Chinese. Her son Forest went into the Navy. Until 1997-'98 there were still military stationed in Arabia, and it was common for the families to have US military personnel over as guests in their home for dinners. The influence this had on kids Forest's age seemed quite common among many Aramco families. Nan's second daughter, Jessica, was on her way to law school when I started writing this book and was considering some sort of position in oil and gas. Of all the kids in their group who grew up in Arabia, many are working in some sort of international sphere.

Nan and I discussed the difference between being raised with a Western education, which promotes a logical left-brained attitude toward tasks, and events we saw in the East that demonstrated the reverse. Nan recalled observing the crews that would come around and sweep the streets in the compound. They would create piles of debris, including downed palm fronds, greenery and miscellaneous stuff, which would blow around in frequent high winds. She watched the crews standing on top of the large piles and simultaneously attempting to pick the piles up and place them in the truck. The street sweepers were from countries like Sri Lanka, Pakistan, Bangladesh and India. Their type of logic seemed so strange to us, and if you didn't develop a sense of humor around this, it would make you cry.

Noel was raised in the 1950s in Guam, the Philippines and also in Hawaii, which at the time was not Americanized and had a greater sense of its own separate culture. Noel believes that she and her siblings were more like CCKs (Cross-Cultural Kids) because they grew up in several differing cultures. In contrast, the Aramco children, while living the definition of "expatriate," were more rooted and grounded in US culture because they were growing up inside an American bubble, the compound, which was surrounded by the country of Saudi Arabia.

Years ago at Aramco, there were no Arabs living on the compound. If you were suddenly dropped from a helicopter into Dhahran in the '70s you would think that you had landed in a housing development in Phoenix, Arizona. The kids were completely surrounded by kids like themselves and participated in all-American activities. As a teacher, Noel has memories of asking one little girl who was as American as apple pie what nationality she was. Her answer was, "I am Saudi." Upon asking a little boy for the capital of America, his answer was "Houston." Nowadays that picture is entirely different since the community is diverse and multicultural, and the students play with all sorts of nationalities.

Noel thinks the Aramco kids were naïve, and I would agree that on some subjects they were. "However, our CCKs in Dhahran were clearly so much more comfortable around adults; they could converse, spend time with and function around adults with ease." Noel suggests that this skill comes from the fact they were so closely monitored by so many adults throughout their lives.

Around the world, millions of kids are being raised as global, not national, citizens. They experience programming to understand the in-between places and peoples that now comprise this beautiful planet. I believe the more we lean into liminal living, the more connected we become to ourselves, to each other and as nations.

Chapter 9

WEDDINGS AS CULTURAL EDUCATION

SAUDI WEDDINGS ARE MAJOR CULTURAL events markedly different in perspective and ceremony from other cultures. The contrast between the expat and Saudi experience engenders much curiosity and, therefore, anyone receiving an invitation to a Saudi celebration felt like an honored guest.

Linda's family arrived in Dhahran in September 1980, almost four decades ago. She was fortunate enough to be invited to enjoy a memorable Saudi wedding. Linda had met Jaffer, a cheerful *Shiite*, at the Dining Hall. He had worked for Aramco since 1946 when he was twelve years old; he learned to speak English well and built good relationships across cultures. He also was willing to discuss local politics, which were normally a taboo subject in what was an isolated, parochial culture in the 1980s, with little exposure to the outside world.

Jaffer was different.

Linda had heard descriptions of Saudi weddings from other expats and had always wanted to attend one. For months Jaffer primed her that she would be invited to his family's next wedding. One day that phone call arrived.

WEDDING BELLS, SAUDI STYLE

In traditional country weddings back then, the celebrations were complete when the groom showed up at the bride's home to claim her. Stories abounded about people being stranded in a Saudi home for several days, wondering if the groom had got cold feet or was rejoicing with his pals so long that he didn't want to break up the party (Saudi parties can last for several days).

Jaffer, like so many Saudis, had two wives residing in the same house, with five children from each. One of his older children was studying in the US. Like so many Saudis, he quickly built an affinity with Americans. However, he was unable to reassure Linda as to how long the wedding would be. He gave her the typical *inshallah* response—meaning the time and conclusion of the celebrations would remain unpredictable. He did reassure her that she would not be alone; other Westerners would be present.

She dressed in a sparkly caftan and evening sandals. Since no men would be present, she could show her arms. She wore gold jewelry as is the custom even in the most modest of households. Jaffer picked Linda up (she was covered for the drive), and they drove out the security gates of Dhahran, entering a different world.

This wedding was a typical country wedding and would be held in the large Shiite suburb of Qatif. They pulled up in front of a walled clay and concrete house. Jaffer deposited her outside the gate where she made her way up to an open door. Linda peered inside; no one was there. Finally, someone came from another room and greeted her in Arabic. Linda handed her the wedding gift, and the gal's smile revealed some missing teeth. Linda says, "I was compelled to follow my own wedding traditions, removing some beautiful copper leaves from my living room wall and wrapping them in wedding paper." But who really knows if the bride ever received them or if the hostess kept them.

The woman said, "*Shukran*," and motioned to Linda to follow her upstairs onto the rooftop. A rather large group of women in long colorful dresses milled about quietly. Spotting three or four expatriate women, who clearly stood out and were also Jaffer's "special friends," Linda made her way over to them. They chatted, got to know one another and speculated about the timing and what might happen next. This was a very alien happening for these Westerners. They even wondered aloud how they would recognize the bride.

Along one wall was a velour chair (perhaps a car seat?) on a carpeted platform. It seemed to be a place of honor. A group of women in abayas showed up looking for a space to set down their drums. They selected a corner, removed their abayas and sat cross-legged on the rooftop. One of the expats presumed they were the local "band" hired from a neighboring village to play for the celebration.

Some very old women sitting down were smoking from hookah pipes. The drums started and rhythms got faster. Saudi women started dancing, the tempo quickened, and they started throwing their heads around flinging their long hair from side to side, backward and forward. Linda was surprised at the seductive nature of the dancing and thought, *All this energy for other women?* This was followed by high-pitched ululating from women all over the rooftop. This was becoming a more *National Geographic* experience moment by moment.

One of the British women joined the dancing, and Linda followed suit. It wasn't long before she too was consumed by the primal rhythms and throwing her hair about. The night was sweltering hot and sweat poured down her back. The Saudi women seemed pleased with Linda's dancing and urged her on by ululating and clapping. The musicians, all old women, smiled, their stained or missing teeth evident, then played even faster. Linda transformed into a whirling dervish!

Later, she realized that Jaffer had provided his family with entertainment in the form of expats. It was not simply a kind gesture to be invited; it was actually a calculated move. The foreigners became the highlight of the evening. When Linda ceased dancing, the onlookers were disappointed. The music subsided at eleven o'clock, then the bride appeared in a long pastel dress and a rhinestone tiara and was escorted to the velour seat. She started to read from the Quran. Women proceeded to bring out bolts of fabric and unfurl them in front of her. The spreading of fabric ensued for a while prior to food arriving on simple round aluminum trays about three feet wide. With no choice but to sit down on the hot rooftop to eat, Linda and her new expat friends joined the Saudi women, who seemed perfectly comfortable with extreme heat.

Fresh goat meat was served. No doubt the animal had been killed that day then prayed over. The rice that accompanied the meat was uniquely Saudi Arabian and delicious. Everyone eats with the right hand, the left hand being considered unclean. Tea was served in small handle-less cups. Sliced oranges were passed around, dinner was completed and calmer drumming ensued. They had danced, the bride had made her grand appearance and finally they had eaten. The only item of business left was for the appearance of the groom to claim his bride.

By now it was well after midnight and the expat women were sleepy. During the hotter months, especially several decades ago, Saudi women rested or slept during the day. They tended to be more active during the night when it is cooler. By this time, the expats were wondering when they would get off the rooftop. They had seemingly exhausted all mutual interests and became subdued. One hour stretched into the next. They observed the band gathering their instruments and noted the bride was gone—finally, the silent sign that the wedding was over. Though the groom hadn't presented himself to the women, he had come for her downstairs and apparently they were off on their new life together.

Linda recalls arriving home around 4 a.m. The question is, was she set up to be the evening's entertainment in the form of an expat performance or was she truly an honored and special guest? Perhaps the answer lies in "yes and." Clearly this was an example of how the Saudi culture was not straightforward and things were seldom as they appeared.

COUNTRY WEDDING

Michelle worked as a nurse at Saudi Aramco clinics. She made friends with the local population easily and mentored several local gals through their nursing training. One gal was a Shiite and invited Michelle to their family home in Al-Hasa for a family member's nuptials. This was Michelle's first Saudi wedding. It was a country wedding with simple village people not a formal high society wedding. Michelle went to the women's tent and was struck by how much the women dressed for each other. These exotic creatures emerged from their abayas to entertain each other, with plenty of cleavage and dripping jewels. Amazing music was created from drumming on large drinking bottles. Several women stood on tables and performed belly dancing.

This wedding also started around 11 p.m. and continued until the wee hours. Michelle remembers getting a glimpse into a village hovel and, by the light of a lamp, seeing two families with the bride and groom plus a mullah. She guessed they were signing dowry papers.

Later, dancing commenced. When the groom arrived to claim his bride, the women rushed in a great flurry for their abayas to cover themselves. The bride and groom sat on makeshift thrones while a greeting line of family and friends formed. Later they all went back to the bride's family house. The couple went up to the bedroom and the entire family waited for them to exit the bedroom. When they did, everyone cheered, jumped for joy and applauded. By now they were family members, and immediate family members could remove their abayas. Michelle recalls that wedding as an authentically alien experience that demonstrated the raw nature of the culture.

UNINTENDED CONSEQUENCES

Michelle also recalls working in the clinic the night many women and girls were brought from a fire in a wedding tent. Someone had brought sparklers that set the tent on fire, and it had only one exit. The women were dressed provocatively and refused to exit the tent without their abayas. Panic ensued, and the burning tent collapsed on more than a hundred women and children. Many died that night and Michelle cared for several of the wounded women at the hospital. It was a tragic night.

I recall the event from the news the following days, together with the resulting outrage and grief we Westerners felt for those women and girls who were trapped. While we could wrap our minds around *how* it could happen, it was almost impossible to wrap our heads around *why* it happened.

FORMAL WEDDINGS

Michelle also had the opportunity to enjoy a more affluent city wedding. At the more formal weddings, staged, elaborate decorations and over-the-top ten-foot-high crystal centerpieces with cakes several layers high were the style. There were gifts on the tables, and rare perfumes were given as party favors (at a country wedding one might receive some sort of local trinket). Flowers are flown in from Holland, and crab, lobster and caviar are frequently delivered from overseas.

All Saudi weddings have similar patterns. Whether a sophisticated city wedding or a rough village wedding, they follow the same map. Women entertain themselves while dripping in jewels and gold, wearing Cinderella-like dresses. Piped music with staged belly dancing and an energetic dance party happens, then a massive feast is served. Old ladies, young girls, in groups and singly, would shimmy and sway in front of other women. Michelle enjoyed and appreciated both events. She commented on the raw authenticity of the country wedding and the aspirational nature of the sophisticated city wedding.

While working as a dental hygienist in the capital city of Riyadh, Terry met a seemingly down to earth and normal woman who invited her to attend her daughter's wedding. It turned out that this patient was the wife of a prince and the youngest daughter of King Faisal who ruled from 1964 until 1975. She came from the northern part of Saudi, and when attending the clinic, she dressed modestly in a plain abaya, not giving off any airs and graces. Terry had no idea she was of royal descent.

Terry was told she was welcome to bring a guest. On the appointed day Terry and a friend pulled out all their best finery, wore every gold bracelet and bangle they could find and arrived at the InterContinental Hotel in her husband's camping Suburban, which seemed somewhat dismal amid a sea of Rolls-Royces.

Upon entering the hotel, they saw a group of women and chose to join them and await instructions. When Terry's dental client showed up, she indicated they were honored guests and must follow her. This normally very plain lady was unrecognizable, wearing a stunning white suit with the biggest real sapphire necklace Terry had ever seen.

The wedding room was like a Cinderella dream scene, tastefully done with white sparkles. They waited for ages, and finally around midnight the bride showed up, a vision of white in a traditional Western wedding dress. Because she had to greet everyone in the room, it took almost an hour for her to walk from point A to B. Each guest greeted her in traditional Arabic style with kisses on each cheek. The orchestra was a female band, of course.

There seemed to be a procession of greetings, and people would just show up in front of Terry and her friend and be hugged and kissed, then in a flurry they would be off. Finally, at 3 a.m. this big whoosh like a wave caused the entire crowd to murmur—apparently, the men had arrived. Out came the abayas. The father, brothers and uncles of the bride together with the groom entered the room, and at 4 a.m. everyone was finally escorted into the banquet room where they ate. Terry finally departed at 5:30 in the morning.

Saudi women really live full-out at weddings. While it appears that much of the Saudi population live simple and somewhat sheltered lives, when women are offered the opportunity for self-expression and a party, they grab it with both hands. I was always surprised and delighted by their passion for social occasions. Their tribal background, huge families and cooperative lifestyle form a framework for hundreds of intense and close relationships.

TYING THE KNOT

Weddings traditionally offer the outside world a glimpse into an intimate relationship through ritual. Saudi weddings offered us, their honored guests, a window into their traditions that would never be seen nor appreciated just by living side by side with each other.

The reports of colleagues and male friends invited to the other side of the wedding were less colorful; for them, the wedding could be extremely long and tedious. The male wedding equivalent is mostly a reception, drinking tea, often some sword dancing and smoking *shisha*, the traditional Middle Eastern water pipe.

These glimpses into a culture were precious and provided insight as to how to interact and bridge the cultural divide we were immersed in every day. In all their variations, weddings told the story of how this mysterious social system functioned.

Part 4
NEW PARADIGMS

Travel is fatal to prejudice, bigotry and narrow-mindedness, and many of our people need it sorely on these accounts. Broad, wholesome, charitable views of men and things cannot be acquired by vegetating in one little corner of the earth all one's lifetime.

—Mark Twain

Chapter 10

NEW PATTERNS AND POSSIBILITIES

IMAGINE THIS: A YOUNG WOMAN, "straight off the farm" as she describes it, flew around the globe in 1959, taking at least three flights to arrive in Dhahran. A brand-new Aramco hire with a pioneering spirit had someone in Dhahran assigned to meet and greet her. Helen's new guardian hastily gathered her up at the airport and unceremoniously dropped her off at her new home since his wife was at that very moment in the clinic and in labor.

"A box," is how she describes her first home. The Swedish-built prefabricated structure was simple, starkly plain and totally unadorned, with not a bit of comfort in sight. It consisted of four bedrooms, a communal kitchen, a living room plus a bathroom.

Her first night in her house she found a cockroach "the size of a camel." She immediately pulled the bed into the middle of the room, took the mattress off and examined every single coil then pulled the dresser in front of the door for protection from other possibly larger intruders.

Helen, sixty years later, is one of the most seasoned expats I have ever met; she seems like a gracious and calm goddess these days. She describes herself back then as naïve, shy and challenged in the face of her first roommate, Edith Quimby, who appeared to be bold, bossy and brash. Her initial welcome included some pragmatic instructions. "If you have men over, I want them out by 6 a.m., and I don't ever want to see them." She then invited Helen "to see how much she could drink."

Helen was overwhelmed, intimidated and confused. Prior to departing the US, her dad had told her, "Helen, if it is not a good place, you come straight home." Helen's initial response was, "But I have signed a contract." However, in the face of such disconcerting circumstances she was aware of the impulse to flee. Helen bottled all this apprehension up. This was an oil company after all and "apparently a really rough crowd." I got the impression she felt she had to buckle down in the face of corporate and personal expectations from the people around her.

A couple of weeks later another employee mentioned that Helen seemed subdued. She inquired whether anything was amiss. Helen confided she was considering returning home. Her colleague, aghast, proceeded to go about the business that expat friends around the globe do for each other over and over. She proceeded to remind her that this was absolutely the best overseas teaching position in the entire world. The parents and students were all wonderful. Supplies were not a problem. The teachers themselves were well taken care of and it was an amazing opportunity.

The value of belonging to a group of people who have been there for years, sometimes decades, is a priceless resource when living overseas. Colleagues and friends on the same journey served as a reminder, when we personally could not remember how good life really was, especially in the face of tough living conditions. Only we can change our paradigms, these invisible rules and forces that live only in our heads; however, friends can be the biggest affirmation of the other side of the coin.

Ultimately this colleague offered Helen a room in a different housing unit. All Helen's belongings got moved over and her life changed rapidly for the better. Her new situation was with a gal in a four-person unit who had the entire place to herself. A perfect solution. This ended up extending Helen's stay in Arabia until 1984– twenty-five years! Helen subsequently married and gave birth to a son, Mark, in Saudi. To this day this elegant lady is a walking inspiration to many others. She stays connected to her friends and acquaintances and is a bright light of hope and positivity. Helen lived a gritty, gutsy life full of adventure and experiences beyond what she would have enjoyed had she returned home to the Plains. Adventuring requires courage.

METAMORPHOSIS

Helen successfully changed her paradigm and quickly. If we consider humans to be like a computer, the paradigm we use is the operating system. It shows up as our perspective, our frame of refer-ence—how we see the world based on information, experiences and beliefs. Almost all of our thinking is reactionary programming we learned from growing up, the society we live in or the faith or belief system we embrace.

Moving overseas required us to transform into expats. We don't arrive as such. Frequently we arrive with willingness. The willingness to be surprised, to change and to learn, and yes, we get to encounter all three in varying degrees. The amount of willingness to change that we bring to the table affects our journey. After pouring ourselves fully into unfamiliar and foreign experiences, it is common to discover that our mindset or our paradigms—and, I believe, our very soul— are changed at depth.

After living so many years abroad, we can turn around and see that we have changed without noticing how or why. New paradigms form silently inside our heads. Having spent 5,472 days in Arabia, I look back and wonder at how frequently I found my life mundane and boring. In the moment, our lifestyle was magical, too, but we rarely appreciated it.

HOW DOES A HOUSE BECOME A HOME?

Nancy, her husband, Bob, and their two daughters landed early one evening in the 1980s and were treated to a cool but pleasant January. Initially they were assigned to North Camp in Dhahran. Their neighborhood consisted of a motley collection of temporary housing in trailers. At that time, dozens of families were leaving due to layoffs within the corporation. Even in Saudi Arabia, living the corporate life meant that at any moment, as business require- ments changed, personnel would be shunted around the globe and, frequently in the 1980s, summarily dismissed and sent home. As a result, the transitional nature of the community was intensified.

Precious housing units were released to new families, but they were neither desirable nor attractive. Frequently mobile homes were used to house new families, especially when the normal compound homes were packed full. There are tales of someone having put a Century 21 real estate sign outside their unit for fun, because how could you "sell" a property you don't own?

Imagine giving up an American home in a lovely tree-lined neighborhood to cross the world and land in a trailer park surrounded by sand and rocks. This was the fate that awaited hundreds of families during many of the oil field boom periods. Nancy's trailer was a single-wide with three tiny bedrooms, one at the far end for parents and two at the other for the girls. In true Arabian tradition, hospitality came first and a sack of groceries was already deposited in the kitchen when they arrived from the airport.

Probably tens of thousands of Aramco employees over the years had the same breakfast on their first morning—long-lasting milk in blue and white boxes (this white liquid seemed to be magical stuff, as it would stay usable for what seemed like years when refrigerated), cereal, orange juice and a plate of homemade chocolate chip cookies.

Nancy felt like this was an auspicious start. Each new recruit was assigned to a greeter, and there was a note from Bob's contact that he would come by the trailer in the morning to pick Bob up and take him to work, and the Welcome Lady would be calling to meet with Nancy. Nancy assumed the Welcome Lady would come in, enjoy some coffee and chat. She was startled by the arrival of Johanna, complete with a bus ready to tour the compound. The girls were fast asleep and had to be aroused quickly, organized and shoved on the bus, where they were immediately taken to school and registered right there and then. There was no time to think about the situation; they plunged straight into the routine.

LOVE IN THE KINGDOM

Sheryl Wright is now living on the Sunshine Coast of Australia, teaching international students English, but in 2000 she lived in Kingdom. She has Saudi males in her class in Australia, and if they are naughty, Sheryl threatens to tell their uncles back in Saudi (it's a tribal society, so chances are she knows someone who knows someone who can actually do this).

Sheryl was recruited in the UK and during her interview was told that the odds of finding a husband in Saudi were very poor. Yes, there were lots of single men in Saudi Arabia: "the odds are good, but the goods are odd." Obviously, this was a reflection of the lack of cultural and feminist sensitivity back then. Nowadays, hopefully, professional women would not be subject to that type of comment. Sheryl approached the idea of going to Arabia as if she were going to be a nun. Of course, the reality proved to be 180 degrees different.

On ANZAC Day (the celebration of Australia and New Zealand's going to war during World War II), there was a party at the British Aerospace compound. Sheryl met her future husband there. He was in party mode at the time. She applied the standardized interview test of six questions that Western single women give men upon meeting them in Saudi: "Are you married? Have you ever been married? Are you still married? How many times have you been married? Do you have a car? And can you drive across the King Fahd Causeway?" The causeway was the highway built in 1986 between Saudi and the island of Bahrain. It is linked by several islands in the middle. We traveled that road frequently since Bahrain was our bolt-hole for parties, drinking, fun and great haircuts. These questions were the trademark of many single women who were longing for more freedom and looking for males who could facilitate that.

Sheryl recalls their first date was at La Gondola, an Italian restaurant in Al Khobar. Her date seemed anxious he might get arrested since he was in the family section, and they were unmarried at the time. Divided seating still applies in Kingdom, with women and families in one area and single fellows in another. This was normal and a facet of every single restaurant until recently. While some restaurants have since combined the sexes by creating one entrance and one eating space, there are still more traditional establishments where the old system of segregation of the sexes is to be found.

Sheryl worked with a Saudi fellow who one day calmly announced he was going to Morocco for the weekend to pick up his new sixteen-year-old wife. It was very matter of fact; he showed Sheryl some photos as if he were going to pick up a new pet or car. His justification for taking another wife was that his first wife had delivered only daughters, and this wife would give him a son. Everything about it was handled as if this was perfectly normal and natural. Apparently, he found a new wife and showed Sheryl a photo of his son before she left. In the West we find this challenging; however, arranged and other types of marriage frequently do produce love. This is not a guarantee, but there are so many ways for love to abound. Another paradigm blown!

UNCONVENTIONAL PLAYDATES

Nariyah was a tiny dot on the map of Saudi Arabia in the 1960s, approximately 144 miles from Dhahran and 106 miles from Jubail on dirt roads that were often impassable because of blowing sand. Imagine an encampment with perhaps forty expats and several other nationalities supporting the community.

The airstrip consisted of a strip of sand that was reasonably flat. The terminal was a small wooden chest containing one single fire extinguisher. Prior to the arrival of the company plane, which came daily bringing personnel, provisions, equipment and everything one could possibly require from civilization, someone had to drive up and down the airstrip to chase away the camels that inevitably wandered onto the runway. Helen's son, Mark, then five years old, was one of only a couple of children living in Nariyah. There were a handful of families with kids, many older than Mark.

Six to eight families lived there. The other children did not stay around much. There was no school and none of the facilities, like swimming pools, tennis courts or recreation centers, that were available on the other compounds. Helen, concerned about Mark's socialization, would plan playdates for him. She would put his name on the manifest for the company plane, and he would happily hop on and fly to Dhahran to visit friends, spend the night and enjoy the privileges of the "big city." The next day his host mum would put him back on the plane to fly home.

This was normal, neither strange nor exotic. They had to deal with life the way it was, and this was Helen's workaround in order to have her son enjoy some socialization, stimulation and fun. Helen took it in her stride.

Ultimately, Helen's family relocated to Abqaiq, a larger compound with ninety-two families. Mark started school there. They created deep friendships that exist to this day, generations later. Helen considers this period an adventure that she still cherishes. Very few Westerners have had the opportunity to live and tolerate such difficult conditions, but Helen reports that she became a brighter, more positive woman.

MODESTY

Developing new patterns also created some funny memories. Linda recalls the birth of one of her children in the Dhahran clinic. She was rooming with a Saudi woman who had the outstanding skill of swearing in multiple languages almost simultaneously. One day as both women, one expat, another Saudi, lay in bed nursing their babies, a male janitor entered the room to mop the floor. Both women had the same instinct, to cover themselves. Linda the expat grabbed a blanket and covered her bare breast, while the Saudi gal grabbed the blanket and covered her face.

Arabia served up a variety of experiences and challenges. In every situation, these women were faced with circumstances that were complex and had to be navigated while considering the culture and environment. No one had imagined or practiced these scenarios; the expats just found themselves in their midst and did their best to respond.

These women did three things: they lived in the moment, stayed flexible and, while genuinely unprepared for each preposterous or peculiar situation, they navigated them all with grace. Being thrown into the deep end of life abroad is where we got to invite new and exciting possibilities we might never otherwise have enjoyed.

Chapter 11

BALANCING CULTURES–HOME AND AWAY

IMAGINE WALKING INTO STORES IN SAUDI around Valentine's Day. There is nothing unique, just business as usual: no red hearts on display, no buckets of red roses welcoming you into a florist or grocery store. Imagine having to get on a bus, drive for thirty minutes and walk around town in a hot black robe looking for a decent-size pumpkin at Halloween; then finally finding it at the third market and discovering the cost is more than fifty dollars! Imagine it's Christmas season and there are no trees in the stores, but you can shop at the local crafts market, and by asking the friendly Filipino fellow–not a Saudi—he will bring out a few paltry Christmas decorations from the storeroom that look like leftovers from Christmas 1969. That all was normal for Saudi Arabia.

Initially I found the loss of traditions and holidays to be the largest source of grief. I believe our souls feel absence, or at the very least, sense a longing for traditions we enjoy year after year. In December 1995, during my first twenty-one days in Saudi, it poured. Torrents of water soaked the land, ran down the streets and flooded the pavement. The drainage was designed for desert conditions, not this deluge. Looking out in horror from steamed-up windows, I was hoping for a glimpse of a Christmas tree, seasonal lights or a group of carolers. As far as Christmas was concerned, we seemed to be in a vacuum.

Our tolerance for ambiguity, together with our ability to be creative, was tested to the max on the subject of holidays in Saudi. Every single Western holiday seemed to have its own set of challenges, from the lack of Easter eggs and candy for Easter baskets to smuggling Christmas trees and ornaments across the Causeway from Bahrain. Every improvisation we devised built our resilience, creativity and ultimately great joy.

We discovered the underground community and attended Christmas service. The fellow with the operatic voice who stood behind us is a close friend to this day. With every Christmas season in Saudi, more personal traditions became established; we built layers upon layers each year, to the point where now we look back and consider those times "the good old days." With time, creativity and good humor, the gap between what was familiar and normal in the West and our new customized version of Christmas 2.0 got built. Eventually the vacuum transformed into magic.

First, we had to learn where the Saudis stood with each holiday—some were more "acceptable" than others. There are layers: the Saudi government's perspective; the Mutawa's (religious police);

what the commercial establishments can get away with; and the feelings of the average Saudi on the street about Christmas, Valentine's, Fourth of July and Halloween.

For the most part Saudis in the 1990s to 2010 were curious, interested and willing to participate, particularly if the event involved entertaining their children. Dozens of SUVs would flood the compound on Halloween; lots of small Saudi children clutching makeshift bags, sometimes even grocery bags for their prospective haul of candy piled out of these SUVs. Nannies, older siblings and parents would emerge and proceed to walk door to door, stopping for candy and conversations. The thrill of seeing them find so much delight in our traditions was eye-opening. However, sometimes the crowds had to be managed and curtailed by a cadre of security guards closing roads and patrolling areas to prevent Saudi teenagers from off camp mixing it up with girls on the compound and other minor infractions.

VALENTINE'S

Valentine's Day was frowned upon, to say the least, by the Saudi authorities. The main governing body regulating these types of activities is called the Committee for the Promotion of Virtue and Prevention of Vice. They take their jobs very seriously. The expat population treats them like fun killers or the Dementors in Harry Potter—basically dark beings who feed upon human happiness. In the case of Valentine's Day in Saudi Arabia, the Committee's job was to prevent red roses from being sold. Retailers would be cautioned to hide anything tainted with the color red. Wrapping paper with red hearts was to be destroyed, and any dreaded cupids, stuffed animals or hearts in store windows were to be removed.

Retailers reported they had been visited by committee members several days prior to Valentine's Day and were threatened that if they sold even one red rose, they could be shut down. At the same time, hundreds of young men would visit the shops to purchase heart-shaped boxes of chocolates from behind the counter. If caught, the shopkeepers would be accused of encouraging these young men.

Practically speaking, attitudes toward Valentine's Day and other Western celebrations drove commercial activity underground. Red flowers and gifts were simply hidden in stockrooms. Anything related—hearts, stuffed bears holding hearts, etc.—would be locked up behind closed doors. A relationship with the shopkeeper would magically open these doors. Store owners were generally willing to sell expats anything, but they needed certainty that you would not turn them in to the Committee. And they priced a dozen red roses at thirty *riyals* ($8) instead of the usual ten.

Stories abounded of Saudi couples being trapped by the religious police as they met each other in restaurants and cafes. Saudi police could check couples for the correct marriage documents to make sure they were authentic and not dating. They were vigilant about clamping down on what they deemed inappropriate behavior in public. These incidents seemed somewhat mythical to me, since I was not exposed to that extremism, partially protected by compound life. I never did witness Saudi Police bullying.

In August 2016, the decision to sentence five Saudi males to a total of thirty-nine years in prison, as well as 4,500 lashes among them, was upheld. Their crime? They had been found dancing with six women they were unrelated to on Valentine's Day. Alcohol and red roses were also seized. This sort of extreme reaction continues to be shocking and tragic. It was the first time I had heard of Valentine's Day being the provocation for violence. Although limitations imposed on us by the strict Muslim regime were evident, our holidays were for the most part tolerated with a "we will look the other way because of who you are, a foreigner" type of attitude. Again, signs of the privilege we enjoyed as expats.

YULETIDE/HOLIDAY/NATIVITY/NOEL—CALL IT ANYTHING BUT CHRISTMAS!

Since the early 1950s and perhaps even before, a Christmas pageant was part of the package in all the compounds. For several years, Mary would arrive on a donkey and Joseph wore Saudi sandals. Real Bedouin shepherds would drive their sheep into the amphitheater and across the stage, leaving fresh deposits that delighted the kids in the audience. Three kings dressed up in exotic finery arriving on real camels produced a high level of glee and liveliness. I found the reenactment of the Christmas story wrapped inside the original environment a mystical gift every single year.

School was out for several weeks over Christmas and New Year's Day. The kids were prepared by the faith groups for Christmas by practicing for the pageant. Since Christmas carols were not played anywhere on the radio or television, the stories and traditions were passed down orally in families, faith groups and the community. Although biblical culture was not encouraged in public, it was nurtured in private. Kids learned carols, recited the bible stories and reenacted these scenes inside the heart of Islam, a conundrum to be cherished for a lifetime.

At one time, decades prior to our arrival, Christmas was celebrated in the streets with joy among the entire community, Arabs and Westerners. But by the time we arrived in 1995 many of these traditions had gone underground. Many perceptions and traditions have transformed over the eighty-five years of Saudi-US partnership.

Tales of Christmases past start with Santa Claus arriving on the compound by various methods of transportation. Apparently one year a US Air Force helicopter was his preferred choice of vehicle. In other years he arrived by golf cart, a fire truck, camel or horse. The entire compound came out to celebrate. Everyone used to turn out on the streets to greet the arrival of Santa Claus. Gardeners from India, Sri Lanka or Bangladesh who were practicing Hindus; educated doctors from Egypt, Syria or Jordan who were practicing Muslims; and the entire constituency of Western Christian families—in short no matter the religion, customs or culture—everyone would turn out to enjoy, laugh with and celebrate Santa Claus.

MODERN-DAY CHRISTMAS PLANNING

Aramco Community Services provided a gift to every child on the compound during the Christmas season. The gifts had to be ordered months earlier or brought in from the West. The system was designed to get age-appropriate gifts for every child whose parents signed up. A corporate-sponsored Santa, who dressed up appropriately in his red Santa suit and was accompanied by several elves who looked and played their parts extremely well, would attend house

parties where several families would gather to share seasonal goodies and celebrations. Expats and locals would offer entrepreneurial
services on camp: bakers, creators, decorators and others marketed
their artisanal wares, from holiday cards and candles to light-up signs
and pottery Santa Clauses. Many of these goods were assembled on
camp, but several months of planning and forethought had to go
into creating these projects. Summertime was a common vacation
season for most families, so orders had to be placed for ingredients
and supplies prior to that. These items were shipped to a location in
one's home country. In the early days we would purchase everything
necessary for a year and return from home to the Kingdom with as
many as eighteen large boxes shipped by air to be processed through
customs in Saudi.

For in-Kingdom seasonal preparation, shoppers' buses picked us
up almost from the door and took us to locations where Westerners
would shop. The bus driver would help load and unload strollers,
kids and shopping bags at every stop. I would often go to old Al
Zamil's on Abdul Aziz Street. The store was filled with crafts and
supplies; Mr. Zamil's wife was American and so had a clue what
Westerners would enjoy. They brought in Christmas decorations
and other things you could not find elsewhere. You had to talk to a
Filipino man, ask for the quintessential "holiday tree" and say certain
things. If you spoke to the right person, they would bring out the
tree in a great big box with CHRISTMAS blacked out. Above all,
we would not talk to the Saudis, although all the Saudis would greet
you when you entered the store with Merry Christmas greetings!
This was a huge surprise compared to what they had prepared us for
at the orientation in Houston.

SMUGGLING

Any forbidden items deemed important to us and smuggled into Saudi grew even more valuable. Plenty of smuggling happened on a low-key level in order to create "home" and host the amazing Christmases we enjoyed. Prior to moving into Saudi we were informed that Christmas trees would not be "welcome." Nevertheless, undaunted, many families would box up a fake tree, wrap it securely in duct tape and call it a dancing pole, a patio umbrella or various other articles. We could also purchase live Christmas trees in Bahrain. A tree carefully wrapped with huge branches and covered up with poinsettias purchased at the international florist shop would be disguised as something else and casually driven through all the checkpoints on the causeway.

One year John and I spent our wedding anniversary in Prague, another year in Vienna. A most special treat was going to the Kris Kringle markets. I brought back many European ornaments and Christmas decorations. One spectacular coup was cramming five miniature live Christmas trees into a small suitcase and successfully smuggling them through customs all the way back to Saudi. I was happy and delighted to gift several of them to friends. The smell of fresh pine in the land where jasmine normally grew was a delightful mix of mischievousness and glee.

Deborah recalls an experience she had in Ras Tanura. Upon walking to her car from the Commissary one day, a fully veiled Saudi lady beckoned her over. She quietly asked if Deborah was "interested in Christmas" to which Deborah responded with a questioning nod. The Saudi woman beckoned her to follow. They arrived at the Saudi lady's house on camp and proceeded directly upstairs, where this gal opened the spare bedroom door. To Deborah's amazement she was staring at about forty assembled Christmas trees. Each had been unboxed and set up ready for this one-to-one marketing effort. Apparently, this gal's cousin or nephew was employed at Dammam port, where shipments arrived and were culled for various and sundry illegal imports—like Christmas trees. This fellow was the quintessential entrepreneur; his relative was well placed to fetch more than market value for holiday trees by living on the compound—one of the fun ways to be in the recycling business in Arabia.

Fake Christmas trees rarely if ever left the Kingdom. They are considered priceless artifacts, and when one family departs, another will purchase or adopt the tree. On our fifteenth Christmas in Kingdom, we counted a collection of around twenty fake trees of all shapes and sizes, and my trove was minimal compared to others who had lived there far longer.

Around 2000, I was in Bahrain for a special dinner at the InterContinental Hotel with a group of women from the compound. The Eastern European waitress overheard us chatting and proceeded to invite us to inspect her Christmas goodies at the end of the evening.

In what felt like an illicit drug deal, we found ourselves in the employee parking lot by the dumpsters with a flashlight, digging around in the trunk of the waitress's beat-up car. She had imported several boxfuls of beautiful, hand-crafted glass Christmas ornaments from Poland. We, of course, thought we had found the motherlode. Right there and then she sold a trunk-full of precious decorations, which we joyfully stashed in big paper bags stuffed with newspaper. Four women then traveled home by taxi at 10 p.m.—the customs fellows were oblivious to the smuggling going on right under their noses.

To this day, each time I trim the tree with these ornaments I remember the sensation of clandestine behavior and the funny story around their purchase.

TOLERANCE ... OR IGNORANCE?

For almost ten years we lived at 311 Nomad Trail in a drab stucco home of adobe design. During our first year there I decided to be creative and make some homemade Christmas decorations. I collected large coffee cans from everyone I could. With help from my enterprising houseboy, Bennie, we cut out Christmas tree shapes on the sides of the cans. He then climbed up on the three roof levels, placed the cans about five feet apart, strung lights inside and between them and weighed them down with stones to prevent the wind taking and blowing them off of the roof.

For every year thereafter, these luminarias lined the roof, glowing and sending the signal that Christmas was being celebrated. We waited to see if anyone from Community Services or any other department would protest—but not a word. The only feedback we received was from a couple of Western military pilots at the consulate who frequently landed nearby. Apparently, those lights were noticeable and impressive from above, but no one else picked up the significance of luminarias being a religious symbol.

Our minds and hearts adapted to the hurdles. Creating a sense of home through creative and mischievous practices became a testament to our resilience and the need for tolerance and humor. We were determined to bring these parts of our culture with us, no matter how flexible we had to be. In many ways we were teaching our children the legacy of our home cultures they would have been unaware of otherwise.

Chapter 12

SHIFTING GEARS

THE HONEYMOON, SADLY, WEARS OFF. There comes a time in every adventure when the novelty, delight and newness wind down and one is left with the stark, bare bones of reality. This experience is like gearing down while driving. Serious emotional and physical adjustments are required.

DRIVING IN SAUDI

Unlike other countries, up until recently Saudi Arabia did not permit women to drive. The mental adjustment and adaptation required to manage this limitation was staggering for many women. The inability to exercise what is considered a basic freedom and to rescind control over our lives was, for me, humiliating, debilitating and frustrating. While driving privileges are granted to women in every other country in the world, Saudi stood alone by practicing oppression and degradation of women's rights. The lack of driving privileges affected the quality of life of every woman in the country to varying degrees; however, that is now all in the past since women were granted privileges to drive in 2018.

A short history of women driving in KSA would reveal that in fact women used to be granted *licenses* to drive; however, it was illegal for them to drive *on Saudi roads*. They quit offering licenses in the 1970s. In 1990 dozens of women were arrested for driving in Riyadh and their passports taken as punishment. Seventeen years later, in 2007, Wajeha al-Huwaider and other Saudi women petitioned King Abdullah for the right to drive. Her brothers made a film that went viral and attracted international attention online.

I was one of a few thousand privileged women living in the larger, Western-run compounds permitted to drive on the compounds. Not only that, but I was doubly privileged by the presence of living with a man, my husband, who had a license to drive and was willing to assume taxi duties, which were sometimes arduous in the face of a busy career. Although limited by the twenty-two square miles on the Dhahran camp and the top speed limit of forty-five miles per hour, I still had the sense of being able to control many parts of my life. I could drive my daughter to school, just a short jaunt away. I could drive to the Commissary to shop, the beauty shop for hairdressing and the gym for exercise classes. At least personal maintenance was possible.

Having lived in the metro Los Angeles area followed by eighteen months driving in Yokohama, Japan, the curtailment of my driving freedom, which up until then I had taken for granted, really hit hard. In retrospect, I now understand that my mental state was evolving as my emotions conformed to the transitional shock I experienced.

Yes, I had known about the ban on driving; yes, I had agreed to it by accepting the contract and going to Arabia; yes, I was fully cognizant of the challenges ahead; and yet, the reality seemed to slam into my system on many different levels. Small daily chores like shopping, taking a child to the clinic or applying for a job became monumental hurdles.

Tooling around in golf carts was the preferred mode of transportation in Ras Tanura. Many times, Lynsey would return by golf cart from playing at a friend's house; it was a delightful treat for her. We were not golfers but did appreciate what an appropriate mode of transportation this was. It reminded us we were living on an idyllic mini-resort.

After receiving the *iqama*, the residence permit that gives one the right and privilege to be living and working in Saudi, my husband received a treasured driver's license. He was at that time blissfully ignorant that he had inadvertently been signed on as part-time family taxi driver for the next fifteen years. We purchased an old Oldsmobile, because why would you buy a brand-new shiny vehicle that would be driven only around the two square miles of compound in Ras Tanura? It was common to see old rickety vehicles being driven by upwardly mobile professionals with multiple degrees who wouldn't consider such a mode of transportation in the West.

WHEELS OF HER OWN

Once someone asked Noel to agree to the following statement: "Well, you wouldn't really want to drive out there, would you?" hinting at the wild driving habits that abound in Saudi. Noel's initial polite response was, "Of course not." However, upon some serious reflection, she changed that to, "heck yes."

Not all single gals shared Noel's perspective. For every single woman I talked to, each has a different story.

Naranjan, a Sri Lankan fellow, worked for several expat families on camp. He drove, repaired, transported and tested cars for a large proportion of the expat population. When Noel decided she wanted to purchase her own car for use on camp, he accompanied her to the dealership where he test-drove her car. Can you imagine how this was both demeaning and frustrating for a powerful, professional woman?

Jody reports that she "had an old junker" to get her back and forth to work and the Commissary. She never minded taking the bus to town or an occasional taxi if she had too much to carry or wanted to return prior to the bus returning. She enjoyed the social life on the buses. Everyone chooses their own framework through which to look at the obstacles.

Even in accidents women weren't granted responsibility.

Deirdre backed her Suburban out of a neighbor's driveway and dinged the front quarter panel of a small Toyota parked across the street. The owner, an unhappy little man, insisted on calling Security despite her most sincere offer to take care of all costs. Security arrived, looked at her and asked, "Where is your husband?" Deirdre told him Chris was at the baseball field. "Why?" the security guard replied, with a straight face. "Go and get your husband. HE was driving the car and I must speak with him." With no wiggle room in this institutional and cultural dilemma, Deirdre got into the Suburban, drove to the ball field and told her husband his presence was required at the scene of "his" accident. Responding to these moments that were so fraught with sexism and assumptions became a skill. Chris quickly resolved the situation with Security and the other owner, but Dierdre felt disempowered.

Sometimes the stress and pressure would drive us ladies to do crazy things. "According to strict Islamic custom, women should not ride bicycles, so my friend and I would sometimes ride around camp in high heels," Nan reports. They also made black baseball caps with gold lamé trim and added Saudi veils to them. A favorite prank was to drive through the security gates wearing these Saudi baseball caps. The guards would look and laugh hysterically. They understood the need for some cultural steam to be blown off. There were tales of gals out washing their cars in spandex and high heels, another silent rebellion against the often oppressive rule that called for us to be appropriately dressed while outside. A certain amount of hijinks was tolerated, but there were definite lines that should never be crossed.

WILD DRIVERS

Saudi driving has earned its reputation as a wild and dangerous free-for-all on the highways. Vickie and her husband were driving into Khobar one evening in the far right-hand lane and were stopped at a red light. The Saudi gentleman behind them wanted to turn right, while they wanted to go straight. He bumped his car into theirs and proceeded to try to push them out of the way so he could make his right turn. On another occasion they were out in the desert one evening enjoying the sunset. A Saudi in a Toyota pickup truck was trying to get up a hill but was not having any luck—he was stuck in the sand. Vickie and friends all got out of their vehicles to try to help push him up the hill. When that didn't work, they suggested that they push him back down the hill to a flatter surface to get a rolling start and gain some momentum. He was confused and kept telling them he didn't want to go down the hill; he wanted to go up. They eventually succeeded in convincing him to go down before going up and were able to get his vehicle over the hill.

Tom reports that while returning from Bahrain via the causeway on a busy evening, cars were bumper to bumper, door to door, some even scraping each other, vying for position in line as eight lanes converged into two near customs. A frustrated gentleman in Arab dress from somewhere behind came forward and rapped loudly on Tom's car window. When Tom rolled his window down to see what he wanted, the man angrily informed him the huge traffic jam was all Tom's fault! "I'm sure he was not pleased when I broke into hysterics," Tom says.

Jannelle recalls an incident that occurred at a stoplight in Al Khobar in the middle lane of traffic. To the left of her car were two left-hand turn lanes. She was in one of the two lanes that were marked to go straight, and there was a right-hand turn lane on the far right. The light turned green, and the guy in the far-right lane gunned his engine and turned left in front of all the other cars. "Happened all. The. Time," Jannelle says. Angela adds, "Red and yellow lights are for foreigners!"

"Generally, the local police do not try to enforce traffic

regulations, so it's anarchy on the roads," Doug says. "The police only made an appearance to clean up the wrecks and carnage after an accident. All too often, the victims would be a large family in an SUV that rolled over at high speed, with the occupants not wearing seat belts and infants not in car seats."

Dottie, her husband and kids were driving back to Dhahran from Ras Tanura, passing a truck in the far left lane. Suddenly a Mercedes-Benz sedan came speeding past on the shoulder in an imaginary lane. Farther down the road, they passed the Mercedes again stopped on the shoulder—he must have run over some debris. "We all laughed and agreed speeding does not get you where you want to go any faster!" Dottie tells me. Great lessons.

Trudy reports that one time her husband, John, was in downtown Al Khobar just before Christmas with their son and two other boys (junior high age); they all went into a store to pick up her Christmas present, and a car hit their parked car. "Police came and told John to go back to camp and drop the kids off and come back to the police station. When he did, he got cited for 25 percent of the accident because, as an expat, if he did not live in KSA, the accident wouldn't have happened," Trudy says. A mystifying moment indeed.

MAKE MY DAY—SEND ME TO THE POLICE STATION IN THUQBAH

Men also had differing perspectives on driving and, just because they had permission to drive on public roads in the form of a valid driving license, that permission did not bestow a joyful or easy experience. Here is Doug's story:

I lived in Dhahran, as an American expat with my wife, Elizabeth, and daughter Maddy for eighteen years, from 1998 to 2016. Women could drive in the large compound but not outside. I'm not sure I even wanted *that* privilege.

Douglas Adams, author of *The Hitchhiker's Guide to the Galaxy*, has wise advice for any seemingly impossible and life-threatening situation: 'Don't panic!' I often said that very loudly to Elizabeth on the rare occasion that she let me drive her into Khobar, the city outside our home in Dhahran. The reason Elizabeth panicked so often when I drove there is: a) she couldn't drive there by law (like she would have fun driving in Khobar even if she could!) and b) 99 percent of the drivers there are suicidally insane and don't care if a passenger dies when they drive too fast. They love to play high-speed thread-the-needle, and drive even faster in the emergency shoulder lane. There is the belief that all things are preordained by Allah, so safety is not the concern of the individual. We had a saying that applies here: 'Trust in Allah but tie your camel to a post.' Note—there weren't many trees around.

I nearly tore up my driver's license and threw away the car keys one bad day out as we approached 'the tunnel of death' on the airport highway. Within fifteen seconds, in two unrelated incidents, cars swerved in front of us going crazy fast, nearly causing us to wreck at seventy miles an hour. We lived to go out another day.

That day was a fine weekend Friday morning. I was driving my family in our seemingly safe Land Rover into Khobar to go shopping at Giant. As an advertising hook, Giant boasted the world's largest shopping cart—about fifty feet high. We had been in Kingdom for about fifteen years, and I still had the courage to take the family out!

We were stopped at a red light at the Dammam-Khobar Highway just before the 'rainbow round-about,' a well-known landmark (there are no proper addresses to guide you to a destination, so landmarks are a must).

The traffic light was about to turn green. BAM!!! We were rear-ended with an explosive jolt. Elizabeth and Maddy screamed. I yelled, 'Are you OK?!' We were wearing seat belts, and everyone seemed to be uninjured aside from the huge jolt and a bit of whiplash. Maddy was crying inconsolably.

I turned on emergency flashers and boldly got out to survey the damage—a crumpled rear bumper and back hatch. The guy who hit us was apologetic. His car was in worse shape with a crumpled front end with steam roiling out of his radiator. He was already on his cell to the police. I wanted my family out of there, so I called a taxi to take them home. I knew it was going to be a long day for me.

We got off the road as far as possible so we didn't get into a secondary collision. The other driver—let's call him Mohammed—spoke broken English. I spoke very little Arabic. He explained that he didn't see me since he was on his cell phone talking to his mother while he was eating his breakfast sandwich. The policeman put Mohammed, who was acting as my interpreter, in the back of his car and wanted me to follow them to the Thuqbah Police Station.

Thuqbah is just south of the more upscale Dhahran Boulevard. Driving into Thuqbah is to see what Saudi was like in the '40s and '50s. The police station was rundown and Spartan. I feared being thrown in jail. Also, I had always heard that when an expat gets in a wreck in Saudi, he's always at least fifty percent at fault no matter what the circumstances. However, I was directed to talk to the police captain in his office. There in the flesh was Saddam Hussein in a Saudi police uniform. He spoke English and offered me tea. Of course, I accepted his hospitality.

The captain was acting as judge in the matter. I was pleased to learn that Mohammed was being assigned a hundred percent of the blame. He was an uninsured driver. I had two choices. The first choice was to take the all-important accident report, get three repair estimates, bring them back to the police station and wait for them to try to extract the money for repairs from Mohammed. Not a good choice, the captain explained, since the chances of that working were slim. The second choice was for me to name my price and wait for Mohammed's brother to show up with cash. I chose that option since they were holding Mohammed until we settled. I asked for 2,000 Saudi riyals, about 500 dollars. I had no idea what it would actually cost to repair the Land Rover.

After a long wait and lots more tea, Mohammed's brother showed up with the cash. I signed papers and left with my accident report. No repair shop would touch my car without that piece of paper. I was stopped at the Aramco Security Gate. 'Do you know that your rear end is crumpled?'

'Yes, I know. I have my paper and I will get it repaired as soon as possible.' After that, most family outings to Khobar were in a taxi. There were fewer screams of panic from Elizabeth. Trips across the causeway in the Land Rover are another story.

DRIVING IN THE DESERT

As constricting as the inability to drive seemed, many of the funniest, most enjoyable and magical moments occurred while driving in the Kingdom. Several years after arriving in Dhahran, we accompanied the Dhahran Scottish Country Dance group out to the desert for a barbecue dinner and dance. About twenty SUVs laden with camping and cooking equipment drove about thirty miles from camp and promptly used the tarp to set up a makeshift dance floor. We hooted and hollered while dancing under the stars on a gigantic tarpaulin that buckled and formed mini-dunes underneath, making dancing in the desert a new sport. Small campfires surrounded the dance floor. The dark desert skies observed these shenanigans from overhead. Sparkling confetti was strewn from galaxy to galaxy.

The following day, prior to departure, all the women got in a huddle. When it was time for the caravan of cars to pull out, we all got in the driver's seats and drove. It was always fun for me to drive in the desert, although John pulled the responsible male card and advised I not try slip-facing (driving the car over the edge of a dune down the very steep side risking a rollover). I credit being alive today to that decision, but I did enjoy slip-facing while others drove.

I also enjoyed the benefits of pipeline roads on that outing. They were washboard rugged, but for the most part flat. That particular day was the farthest I ever drove off camp–perhaps a total of sixty miles—and it was such a joy. Seven years later we took our daughter on those pipeline roads to practice her driving while she was home from boarding school. The freedom to drive on paved highways and any road I can find in the US is not often lost on me.

People would frequently get lost or break down while driving in the desert. The environment was brutal and demanding. There were miles of desolation with few main roads at the time. Many of the subcontractors, who were Third Country Nationals from India, Bangladesh or Pakistan, were without transportation or resources and fell victim to the environment. Often they tried to walk into town or take a walk in the desert, and it was common for someone to become disoriented when they strayed from the road. Few if any survived.

Another common danger was hitting a camel on the highway at night. Dark twinkly skies, a barren featureless landscape, open roads and speed contributed to many accidents and, sadly, in most cases both the driver and camel died.

DRIVING TODAY

In a breathtaking move, on September 26, 2017, King Salman issued an order that paved the way for women to commence driving in Kingdom in June 2018. Uber and Careem (a Dubai-sourced driving service) have been hiring, training and preparing women to be drivers since then.

When I talked to Miriam in August 2018, she had just arrived home after driving from the gym (driving is still a novel adventure with the advent of the recent freedoms granted women). On the subject of women driving, she says, "If everybody follows the rules, we will be in peace." Many of the women in Saudi have had their driver's licenses in other countries, so they know how to drive properly. They drive slower in the right lane, they signal before changing lanes, etc.

There have been lots and lots of accidents since the advent of women driving in Arabia, however. There is a tendency for many to blame the new drivers, when in fact they are the competent and sane drivers on the roads now. Miriam talks about the crazy young male drivers. Driving on the shoulder, passing at high speeds in the slower lanes, not observing the signs and switching lanes with no signaling are common events. "These young men may not care about us or other people, but they care about themselves and their cars," she says.

"You get used to being driven, to sitting in the back seat, being on the phone, the laptop, listening to music," she comments, referring to the driving ban. Even her brother, a safety engineer who graduated from Manchester University and had been back for eighteen months, would like to have a driver. Their parents live in Ras Tanura and he is a Sadara (Aramco chemical subsidiary) employee. He has to drive on the Abu Hadriya to Jubail highway daily, which is dangerous and exhausting. "You know what, sister, I wish I could get a visa for a personal driver," he has said to her.

Now will women driving be an easy and straightforward transition? That is doubtful, because the question of women driving brings up so many other cultural and traditional perspectives. Everyone has a unique opinion, and many women will choose to keep their drivers, preferring to spend their energies elsewhere. No matter what, the sociological and economic repercussions will reverberate throughout the Kingdom.

DRIVING AWAY

Chris and Deirdre were pretty quiet on their final exit-only drive over the causeway. No "This is the last causeway line," comments. But after they were comfortably settled in their business class seats and wheels up, they turned to each other with their glasses of champagne and toasted TWENTY YEARS IN SAUDI WITH NOT A SINGLE MOVING-CAR ACCIDENT! That was remarkable and felt like a worthy achievement.

"We sold our dear old Suburban to a family who lived off camp and claimed to be in dire need of a good, safe family vehicle," Deirdre says. "We sold it to them for a song after hearing their long, involved sob story." About a week later they spotted it sitting on a used car lot for sale for 10,000 more riyals ($2700). While this was shocking, bargaining, wheeling and dealing are part of the Saudi mindset.

"We were on the causeway leaving for Bahrain and traffic was horrible," Peter recounts. Frequently the drive over the causeway took several hours due to the paperwork, number of immigration and customs booths and huge amounts of traffic. "It had taken us about two hours to get past Saudi customs. Our driver pulled to the side so he could use the washroom, but he didn't pull over quite far enough and was partially blocking a lane. He ran inside and left the engine running. All of a sudden a stranger, a Saudi man, jumped into our car." His intention was to move the car out of the way, but there was no explanation or communication.

Peter jumped out of the car and pulled this man out of the driver's seat, not knowing what the guy intended. Needless to say, "We went right to the bar at the Ritz when we got there. A crazy final day in Saudi!"

Whether men, women or children, we all lived in Arabia with differing stories and reactions to driving. Whether we were females banned from driving or males who either enjoyed or hated driving there, we left with memories of journeys we might not have survived. In my first month in Ras Tanura, a woman I met only once was killed by a Saudi policeman who hit her on the passenger side on a roundabout. From that moment on I was conscious of the fleetingness of life. Sights of children sitting on Dad's lap while he drove the giant SUV with no seat belt or male fifth graders driving their mums to appointments, barely able to see through the steering wheel, were frequent. The underlying approach to life in Arabia was one of *inshallah*; it was entirely Allah's will whether we arrived at a destination—or not.

When flying on the national airline or the company jet, they played the recorded Arabic prayer for protection. This always reassured me, and I wondered how many, if any, of the wild drivers practiced and played the prayer for protection in their heads prior to getting on the road.

One thing is for sure. I am grateful for the divine protection we enjoyed. As our thoughts began to move toward transition, I realized that the day-in, day-out driving challenge would be one of the most welcoming factors back in the US.

بيت

Part Five
RE-ENTRY

There are two great works for heroes and heroines to perform. The first is to withdraw from everyday life.... The second work is to return to everyday life, carrying the knowledge we have gained in the depths and putting it to use to redeem time and society.

—Jean Houston

Chapter 13

COMING OR GOING

TODAY THERE IS A "LEAVING SAUDI ARABIA" sign near the causeway to Bahrain, and getting your picture taken at the sign is a farewell ritual.

The majority of us arrived with the fullest intention to return "home." In the fifteen years I lived in Saudi, I don't recall meeting more than twenty people who had no intention of ever returning home, who were destined to remain global nomads. When signing on with Aramco, we went with the intention of building financial security, enjoying an adventure and recycling ourselves back to home. I guess perhaps 90 percent or more of us achieved that vision. However, even the idea of "home" transformed along the way. As Aramcons, mostly we lived a fixed and settled existence in a mini-American compound chasing a big dream called "retirement."

We poured our most precious commodities, time and energy, into awaiting that magical moment. While a few counted down the days until they were released from such purgatory and their "real life" could commence, for the most part, we grabbed the opportunity for travel and adventure.

From the moment we left our home in California for what was to turn into eighteen years overseas, I was aware there would be a time when I would return, like a salmon to familiar waters. Whether that would be to a physical or emotional place, I never gave much thought.

Leaving a place looks like it is a one-day simple process. You buy a ticket, put yourself on that plane and voilá, you arrive. Not even close! The reality is very different and more complex—especially when abandoning a foreign life where you have lived and loved through many seasons. Preparing to leave involves both the insidiously hidden and blatantly obvious parts of a process that is an *evolution* rather than an *event*.

We frequently consider a move to be a simple transaction involving relocating ourselves (our physical bodies) while discounting the logistical, spiritual and emotional parts of the process. It's easy to disregard the energy and time required to process the massive amounts of hidden changes that are happening. As humans we are oriented in a physical body, and it's our nature to pay attention to those first.

EXIT ONLY

The exit-only process to depart Aramco is lengthy and complex and requires much paperwork and many surprising activities.

Leaving actually started the first day we arrived in Kingdom.

Because we were living an institutionalized life and were about to be untethered from the mothership, there were layers upon layers of bureaucracy. The logistical and administrative side of departure for many involved a six-month process of paperwork with probably forty different activities. There were forms to complete John's employment with Aramco. Company housing required that we have the house and garden inspected. All cars, boats and other vehicles owned while in Kingdom had to be sold and the documentation presented. There were many urban myths of people stuck in Kingdom while the mammoth bureaucracy held up their exit-only visa stamp—that one final goal in the passport—due to a car or truck from years back not being properly transferred.

Forms a mile deep were required to complete your health experience at the Aramco clinic. I received physical CDs with all my health files, X-rays and CAT scans. By the time I required them and looked closely, which was almost a year later, I discovered they were blank. My entire health history for fifteen years just disappeared. Fortunately for me, I seem to be healthy; however, this could have been disastrous for a person with a tricky history of health issues.

Management of a benefits package was required. Aramco was generous, and HR had systems to ensure each person left well informed of their options. There was a conference to review benefits and the way forward as newly minted annuitants, the term for retirees. This was not a re-entry coaching or preparation session, but more like a high-level snapshot of life in that moment. Although we attended the conference while brimming over with emotions and excitement, this was a corporate experience and feelings were barely mentioned. This was certainly neither the place nor time to start processing the invisible side of our global adventure.

Compared to many global assignments, the Aramco culture invites longevity. Many friends lived there for more than thirty years, embracing a lifetime of experiences. Their children were born in Kingdom, raised in Kingdom, then attended boarding schools and in some cases returned to the Kingdom to work. Several families carried on the dynastic tradition throughout three or more generations. Generational and intercultural living became institutionalized and a clearly defined lifestyle.

The natural re-entry coaching for this group consists of people sitting around and verbalizing their dreams. Groups of us chatted about our dream houses, nest eggs, future hunting, fishing and skiing expeditions. We would dream of places we would visit and the terrific life our kids would have. In hindsight I came to understand how supportive your tribe overseas really is; they were like an echo chamber feeding our dreams back to us. I understand now what a terrific resource they were in offering ordinary ways that kept our visions intact. We were doing this for each other all along, without even knowing it!

The Aramco exit interview is essentially a mini-logistical debrief. Questions like, "Where are you bound?""What is your plan?""What are your aspirations for the future?" Etc., etc., etc. For me it was a cursory and dissatisfying experience, but what did I expect? While it invited me, the "dependent one," into the process in a way I had not felt invited since the interview process eighteen years prior, it left me with a sinking feeling. Exactly what would I pack up and carry with me that would fully describe the last eighteen years?

Freedom, I thought. *What exactly will that mean?*

It was never our intention to remain in Arabia for fifteen years. Like most, we had arrived with a five-year goal on our horizon, but we enjoyed it so much, we stayed for fifteen. Immigration to Arabia is the furthest thing from most internationals' minds, although if you are prepared to convert to Islam and are married to a Saudi national, there are definitely pathways available.

Aramco had been an all-encompassing source of well-being for us for almost two decades. This would be our fifth and last move with Aramco. While there was a sense of joy and looking forward mixed with the dough of creativity at work in my soul, there was also a sense of dreading the cutting of the umbilical cord. The institution had provided our housing, security, finances and society. In the future, we would not have "Mother Aramco," as many expats were fond of calling the company, to call on to fix the plumbing, provide health care, take care of our security and generally protect and nurture. No more 939, a Community Services number we could call at the drop of a hat to have something fixed at no charge. What a privilege that was!

Vaguely disquieting comments would land on the subject of the return to "normality." It would be an adjustment, they said. It might take years to settle, they said. It might involve some grief, they said. There would be a honeymoon period followed by peaks and valleys, they said. Eventually, we would settle, they said. Our lives would never be the same, they said.

We were prepared to create a new adventure. I had some ideas before I left about what that might look like. We understood we needed a plan and a place to live, and then picking up the red thread of our lives would naturally happen ... right? We had friends who were former Aramcons in the town we were moving to; in fact, our next-door neighbors from our first-blush experiences in Arabia were in the same town. We had become connected through our dogs. Our very nosy dog had sought to meet their very protective Ava, and twenty years later we had the privilege of pet-sitting for them.

Our daughter was off to start her university life on the West Coast; we had a beautiful, even magical piece of property and a dream home farther north on the same coast, together with vibrant health. What could possibly go wrong? Mentally, we were somewhat prepared, and yet, the intellectual process of knowing something and living through it are so different that we might as well not have known any of it. While we lived to tell the tale, little did we know in the preparation to launch stages how circuitous the path was going to be, nor where it would ultimately take us.

I studied all the multicultural and re-entry issues books, including Craig Storti's *The Art of Coming Home* and *Third Culture Kids* by Ruth Van Reken, David Pollock and Michael Pollock. I considered the re-entry from the perspective of our nuclear and extended family and sought to prepare myself in the context of a mother, daughter, wife and a trailing spouse, which by that time was my biggest identifier. I thought I was prepared: read the books, studied the literature, stayed in touch with friends who had gone before, paid close attention to my emotions. I was determined to get it "right." If this move were an exam, I was about to score an A+.

TRANSITIONS

On May 21, 2008, King Abdullah bin Abdul Aziz Al Saud

came to the compound to participate in the celebration of Saudi Aramco's 75th anniversary. The eighty-four-year-old King arrived by bus, on inshallah time. Through crowds of cheering people from all around the globe, together with a phalanx of Saudis, he walked, waved, chatted and blew kisses the entire time. Surely this King was beloved throughout the Kingdom, unlike some of his predecessors. From gardeners to science PhD graduates, technology gurus and children from the Dhahran schools, it seemed like the entire world stopped to pay homage to a relationship. Security obviously was very tight. Dozens of uniformed members of the Saudi Arabian National Guard walked casually with the King and his retinue.

A large portion of the community had been feverishly preparing and rehearsing for this moment for several weeks. Friends had been practicing Saudi sword dancing in order to reenact a scene from 1947 when the original King of Saudi Arabia, King Abdul Aziz (ibn Abdul Rahman ibn Faisal ibn Turki ibn Abdullah ibn Muhammad Al Saud), visited the compound and met local children and employees. Several of those very children, now elderly, were honored guests of the King, having returned to the Kingdom in 2008 to re-enact that moment. They had flown halfway around the globe to revisit memories and their connection with the country. For most, it was a lifetime honor and highlight. Even the King treated it as such.

Friends and colleagues participated in a stage production, wearing vintage dresses and hats they'd bought. The transformation to the 1940s was incredible. Children and adults, expats and Saudis, including King Abdullah, danced and celebrated together. Children who called the compound home in 2008 sat on a carpeted stage in front of a huge mural printed with pictures of the children who had attended the 1947 event. A collective sense of well-being was created between the corporation and employees, and more important, the event created a culture bridge.

The baseball field had been converted to an open park area with enormous billboards of photographs from that auspicious day in 1947. The elders walked past those billboards on their way to the staging area marveling at the beautiful memories they evoked. A visceral sense of rejoicing was felt throughout camp. All the participants were thrilled at being in the midst of a royal Saudi celebration—an over-the-top extravaganza.

What was at the heart of this gathering was a celebration of creativity, courage and innovation built over four generations. Tens of thousands of people from all walks of life, in partnership, had built this grand intercultural experiment called Aramco, which in turn ultimately supplied much of the fuel to support countries around the world in becoming more prosperous. This behemoth had transformed itself from a tiny desert oil production company to a world-class energy and petrochemical corporation. Each person—woman, child and employee—was being acknowledged for the small part they played in this global machine.

DISLOCATION

But where was I while all these celebrations were in full swing? Well, I was at home sitting in front of a screen creating a long, boring inventory list of our furniture, household goods and possessions. Yes, I missed the single largest cultural party in the Kingdom during our tenure, one that would probably not be reenacted for twenty-five years—if ever. Rather than living in the moment, enjoying this momentous gathering, I was back to playing the "liminal living" game. Preparing to leave yet hoping to stay. This exact situation is where so many of us in the global mobility lane and throughout the international corporate world frequently land. This was the beginning of our re-entry.

Backtracking slightly, in 2005 we had purchased a home in Bellingham, Washington, in the beautiful Pacific Northwest of the US. Retirement was imminent in 2006, but John had been the beneficiary of two one-year extensions at the time of the King's visit in 2008, so we had one foot in two countries. (The official retirement age for everyone at Aramco was sixty, and to extend beyond sixty required the approval of Aramco's president.) The King's visit coincided with a major shift for me. Discomfort, confusion and a sense of dislocation from my life culminated during this time. We hoped to remain for two more years, so Lynsey could complete high school at the same boarding school, and we could enjoy a few more adventures on our list. Would we remain in Kingdom within our sweet nest of cultural bubbles? Those bubbles had become a stabilizing force through some challenging times.

Ultimately, we lived with this mystery from 2006 to 2010, so the days surrounding the King's visit are a haze. I remember irrational mood swings and fuzzy thinking. Spreadsheets with values attached to personal belongings ruled the day. I felt like my possessions owned me rather than the opposite. Decisions and lists of what to keep, what to leave behind, what to sell and what to donate ran around our heads. I was bored and agitated by the process and the need to balance two possible realities. The only parts I could control were my thoughts, attitudes and preferences. In between wondering if and when we would depart was concern about the logistical details. Flights would have to be booked. Where would we spend the summer? Our Bellingham house was rented until September. What activities did Lynsey have planned? How could we support her; would we have to move her? Would we consider pulling her out of school? And just how would we make all these decisions in a few short weeks? We were living in the land of confusion.

WHEW—HERE WE GO AGAIN

Eleven days later, on June 1, John reported that he was transferring to another project, temporarily relieving much of the stress. Yet another chapter in his Aramco career was starting. Deep breath, a cascade of relief. I felt a mountain of stress evaporate. I also had some major awakenings. Truly there was going to be a final exit from this camel lane. Exactly how would I make these days count from now on? Henry David Thoreau wrote, "I wanted to live deep and suck out all the marrow of life." It was time to get down to business, think through some priorities and values and re-envision how we would like to complete our time in the Kingdom. What else did we hope to accomplish?

I needed to become a sponge of the tolerance, graciousness and hospitality of the Saudi people. Weeks of foggy thinking, confusion and vacillation between anxiety and boredom ultimately fell away in the course of the next few months. I started to deploy some serious daydreaming about what else I wanted out of our Middle Eastern magic carpet affair and how to finish well.

I shifted. We moved houses, threw away excess junk and stream-lined our household. Being in action was freeing. I met women in different orbits, compounds and interest groups. Several professional friends had resigned from full-time jobs and we spent more time together. Although John was traveling the world examining think tanks for KAPSARC (a new venture intended to help with the country's energy strategies), somehow we managed to create a new rhythm that carried us throughout those remaining twenty-four months in Kingdom. Filling my time with Tai Chi and art classes and editing the Dhahran School's yearbook, together with travel-ing back and forth to the US where Lynsey was in school, kept me fully engaged and very happy. Years later, those weeks of turmoil, uncertainty and dislocation were ultimately to become fodder for a re-entry curriculum.

What is the point of adventure if we don't actually grow into or become a more substantial person? Those final two years started to reveal just how magical, mysterious and mystical our stay in Arabia had been. I felt like I was standing under a shower of gratitude.

Chapter 14

READY, STEADY ...

HAD A CRYSTAL BALL BEEN AVAILABLE back then, we would have seen that the next two years we were about to live through were going to be two of the best years, not only of our time in Saudi but of our lives in general. We were about to launch new adventures we would savor for a lifetime.

In the rearview mirror, those two years appear as part of a charming Magic Kingdom life. My brother-in-law Rob would arrive in November for the birding adventures discussed earlier. My dad visited Saudi twice. Having served in the Second World War in Palestine, Israel and Syria, he was distressed by the Iraq invasion which was, in his humble opinion, destroying a precious part of our world. He was nervous about the Iraq War being so close but was willing to come to Saudi anyway. Always up for adventure, from a

Sunday drive to a trip across the globe, he impressed upon me at an early age the benefit of travel and adventure—thus I had welcomed Life in the Camel Lane.

Dad's first visit was during the 2009 Aramco Reunion where I organized a home tour featuring six homes across the compound. Annuitants, people who had worked and retired from Aramco, had returned to the Kingdom and were curious to see either their old neighborhoods or visit their former homes. Many returnees had become local legends in their own right in the community. Gratitude was written all over their faces during the reunion.

By the time Dad visited Arabia, he was widowed, enfeebled and fragile. With macular degeneration in his only good eye, he was quite deaf and walked with a walker. Nevertheless, he wanted a purpose and was keen to walk Kumi, our Havanese dog. Leaving our house, he would walk around the block with Kumi on a leash. If I moved the car, he would not recognize the house and continue walking. More than once a neighbor spotted him and guided him home, and a few times friends called and reported helping him unravel Kumi's leash, which had gotten tangled around his walker. Even the gardeners and houseboys knew him and would say they saw "baba" or "sahib" today. Our diverse and different community seemed to wrap their arms around this old man, and he reveled in that sense of well-being.

On his last visit prior to us departing the Kingdom on our exit-only visas, Dad wanted to extend his vacation six weeks longer than planned. His medications would run out, and there could be dire consequences. A friend of ours, a Canadian ER doc, looked at Dad's prescriptions, interpreted what the Saudi Arabian version and dosages might be and ordered them; we picked them up at the pharmacy, all at no cost. This was a classic example of how the *wasta* system worked—so much more was accomplished through relationships than processes—plus a lesson in the mightiness of generosity of spirit all the way round. A mighty petrochemical behemoth on the one hand, a welfare state on the other, Aramco was a beautiful conundrum that straddled both realities.

After Dad's visit, I felt more prepared to start our exit-only process not just willingly but with full-on enthusiasm, the end, the finale of a grand adventure. I had arrived at a place of eagerness to move on, to prepare for repatriation to America and life beyond Arabia.

For several generations, foreigners working in Saudi were refused permission to return after their departure. "Final" truly meant the end. They were never, ever to visit their old home, their neighborhood or birthplace. They would never walk down the back lane to their best friend's home or wander the *jebels* they hung out in as teens. Departure was fully final and irrevocable. Nowadays, the Kingdom is more open, and company-sponsored reunions are held there every few years. With the recent addition of tourist visas, this should facilitate occasional visits. I wonder how many annuitants will take advantage of this without personal invitations and company support, because it's the people who made the experience, not solely the place.

I made myself think about what *final* meant to me. What were the gold nuggets I had learned, what would I really be taking home and how best could I manage the emotions? Many of us think of re-entry as an *event*, but it's actually more like a tunnel and our new life the light at the end. It takes time to get there.

LOGISTICS

After selling cars and taking care of home inspections, paperwork and exit interviews, we finally arrived at the packing. Packing was climbing a mountain of fifteen years of memories, collections and belongings. Over our allotted five or six days, every piece would be examined, handled and organized into containers. The packers were all TCNs, men who had families back home in distant countries, people whose lives could be contained within ten of these boxes, and here we were with several hundred. I noticed I felt somewhat shamed and spoiled by the abundance we enjoyed. As is customary in Arabia, we fed, celebrated and honored these guys every way we could think of. An old toy—who had a kid that age who could use it? Clothing—whose wife might this fit? Food—do you like to eat such-and-such? Making a game of packing helped soothe any sense of discord. The packers were cheerful to the point of being enthusiastic. I have a sneaking suspicion that their Eastern minds were thinking, *Thank goodness I am not tied to material possessions like these Westerners.*

Shopping mattered, the last-minute dash, a built-in rite of passage for those final table covers, souvenirs or reminders of our lives in Arabia. The last and final trip to our favorite tailor, the gold souk, Desert Designs, the shoe fellow Abdullah, the watch store and the rug store. The preliminary goodbyes and then final goodbyes. A final trip out in the desert to stare at the magnificent heavens, a final very rushed trip into the mall for memories we forgot might be important. While making the move meaningful was the goal, our possessions were a huge part of carrying our home like a turtle back to our homeland.

The sound of tape strapping boxes and the boxes being dragged across tile accompanied the sense of packing up our joys, hopes and gratitude. I recall thinking that the boxes were not full of things but of reminders of the people, places and days we had spent in downtown Khobar or distant trips we had taken.

Here are a few packing moments: Phyllis recalls that she and her husband had to store their cash and passports somewhere in a different part of the house that was a non-packing zone, for fear the packers would sweep them up in their path. Stories of trash cans full of rubbish and other disposables being packed up are frequent. Ron instructed his packers, "Don't pack the tablet," but they ultimately had to unpack the packed iPad twice. The first time it was found in the last box of fifteen boxes sitting out on a hot driveway. The following day, they had to drive out to the warehouse where the boxes were being stored. After searching for three hours, they retrieved said iPad, and once again in the last of twenty searched boxes. These stories abound, and they happen partly due to the rapid nature of a pack, differences in culture and language and just the sheer challenge of keeping one's eyes on as many as eight packers working in several rooms simultaneously.

Packing requires organization, planning and attention to detail. It helps to apply a sense of humor. I recommend mindful moments throughout the day and taking deep breaths. Sitting outside away from the melee listening to the birds for twenty minutes was strong medicine for the upheaval.

However, packing the invisible golden nuggets is so much more important. The upbeat, positively adventurous perspectives that everyone around us infused life with, those were the nuggets.

GRATEFUL FAREWELLS

Key behaviors were saying goodbye to people who made our stay in Arabia not merely bearable but delightful. Our houseboy came until the very last day, the sound of his keys hitting the kitchen counter the perennial signal to get the housekeeping in gear for the day. Sunil and Papu at the Hobby Farm restaurant knew exactly what our orders would be the moment we walked in. The Hobby Farm had become the local version of Cheers, "where everyone knows your name," without alcohol. The list of farewells contained colleagues, personal friends who had transformed into family and the characters who had taken care of us while in Kingdom. I recall the perpetually smiling fellow at the dry cleaners from Sri Lanka; Dining Hall staff; Layakath, who took care of our horses, Shaiboo and Breezy—he had almost assumed the position of spiritual guide, his calmness a constant gift. Ahmed, the security guard on the back gate who over the years offered between five and ninety camels in exchange for our daughter in an ongoing joke. Verbally expressing feelings of gratitude, recalling years of fond memories and wishing them future blessings, were graceful rituals that honored all of us. Each of them expressed real sadness. They, too, lived in the knowledge that one day they would be the person leaving. The goodbyes assumed a pattern of their own, like the dismantling of a mosaic.

There were raw moments with friends who were now extended family, neighbors with whom we had traveled and shared exotic experiences. People wrote farewell messages on poster board we still treasure today. Ritualizing our goodbyes was cathartic, and I believe provided a good runway on which to land well and start afresh.

A TOAST TO OUR DEPARTURE

Back then, the Kingdom of Saudi Arabia appealed to intrepid souls. Living there gave us a taste of 1920s Prohibition in America, with no alcohol openly available. Restaurants were divided into family sections and male sections, so females and males could not socialize in public. Separate entrances were built for each gender, and many of the public and corporate buildings were designed without restrooms for women. Even workshops were conducted with curtains down the middle of the room to separate the sexes.

Movies were cut; all kissing, bared skin and drinking were conspicuously absent. Music was rarely heard downtown. Secret lists and passwords were needed to enter compounds where concerts were being performed. Valentine's, Easter and all Christian celebrations were *haram* (forbidden).

Although these circumstances could lead to bitterness and frustration, for the most part they became tools and a foundation upon which to build resilience, creativity and tolerance. Who would have imagined that living with these limitations and with such a lack of freedom would translate into such a positive, magical and mystical experience?

EXIT ESCAPADES

On my final day in Kingdom, about eighteen of us gathered at the coffee shop for one final fare-thee-well get-together. I was "exit only" in a few short hours. Many were about to head out of Kingdom within the next two weeks for long repats and extended travels. This was my tribe, my rock, the witnesses to my coddiwomple through

Arabia. Friends, colleagues, Hobby Farm mums, Tai Chi partners, theater group members–you name it. Their stories and my story were coming to a fork in the road.

My friend Helenka had kindly loaned us her car for our final week in Kingdom after ours was sold. Well-schooled in champagne brewing, we had a few bottles left and I had intended to share them. The best brewing zone in our house was under the sink in the bathroom next to Lynsey's room. Frequently Lynsey would awaken to a loud *pow, pow*, realize that it was our mad chemistry/brewing experiment and roll over to go back to sleep.

In my haste to complete all the logistics I had forgotten that several bottles were in the back of this borrowed station wagon on a blisteringly hot day in the month of June, with temperatures of almost 120 degrees. I had also forgotten to invite my friends back to the car to give away these liquid treasures. The explosion was inevitable. Being caught with booze on company property, even with an exit-only stamp in my passport, was not the ending I was going for!

Hastily I pulled into the parking lot by the golf course and, with Lynsey's help, gingerly grabbed the knotted grocery bags, each with one bottle, and carried them carefully and calmly about twenty feet before dropping them into the tall garbage cans to explode safely in their own time. I mopped up the fragments from the two bottles that had exploded and hoped that the smell in Helenka's car would fade by the time she returned from vacation.

This small incident speaks to the greater journey, in that some of the joy and mischievousness we got up to in Arabia was behavior driven by cultural dissonance. Saudi remains a dry country. Hundreds of former colleagues harbor stories about the hijinks required to get around the rules of Prohibition. Although we followed the rules for the most part, we never adopted our host country's values, nor did we relinquish our own. We effectively created a new blended culture and learned to balance pragmatism with minor rule breaking.

TRIANGLES

In the 1970s one of the Mission Societies came up with a great analogy that many journeyers around the globe now take great comfort in. Based on their research and empirical evidence with hundreds of missionaries who had returned from the field, they created this theory.

The story begins with a person growing up in a square world. This person is in fact a square, meaning they identify and belong to the ideas and culture of a square world. Square person then moves to a circle country where the food, religion, traditions, language, culture and beliefs are quite different. During their time in the circle world they change at depth, perhaps they eat the food and learn to speak the language of circle world. Nevertheless, they never become or transform into circles.

Ultimately, when journeyers move home or to the next destination, they discover they have lost some of their squareness and have transformed into triangles. They no longer fit one-hundred percent into their old culture—they have changed into a new shape. Triangles have points, and people who have lived overseas and developed new mindsets have new points of view with which to process life. While this theory is simple and easy to embody, it also settles well into the souls of many of us who have left our home culture and then returned.

BLENDING IN

One of the most painful tricks of reality for a repatriated citizen can be the loss of identity or the appearance thereof. In Arabia for fifteen years we had stood out as white, speaking English and even wearing clothing that distinguished us. Standing out was a way of life; on our return, the cultural message in America was changed to "blend in; don't stand out."

We returned "home" to Bellingham. The part of me that was accustomed to being the foreigner, a white face in a sea of brown, was accustomed to standing out. I found that part of myself was now at war with the part of me that wanted to blend, to be accepted. Yet, accepted into what? Once again, I was back to looking for my tribe, wondering where all the people were, since Bellingham was the friendliest place, but just like Ras Tanura when we first arrived, there didn't seem to be a lot of them around.

The people looked like us, except they were hardly like us at all. I observed that almost none of the women in my age group colored their hair. We attended events where everyone was a sea of gray, wearing Birkenstocks and dark-colored Northwest styles, which are fashionable à la REI, but not the height of fashion in Europe or the Middle East.

Although most Saudi women wore abayas, if you could read even the basic ABCs of fashion, you could interpret what classification of clothing was being worn underneath. If nothing else, the accessories told the story loud and clear. The socioeconomic status, background or tribe of people in Arabia was written all over them. We quickly came to subconsciously read the signals—*oh, a Gucci purse; ah, Prada sunglasses*—or we noticed, for instance, that an older, heavier woman's feet were leathery and worn. None of those sorts of cues was available in Bellingham. One of the products of globalization around the world is that socioeconomic status is now couched in a uniform of jeans and sunglasses.

Feeling completely foreign in a place I told myself I should fit into was confusing. I loved the physical place, the geography, the greenness, the huge trees, the water, the lake, Puget Sound ... water everywhere we went, everywhere we looked, eventually so much water I felt my soul was drowning in it.

People would ask where we had just moved from and when they heard "Saudi Arabia," they were stunned. Either no more questions would ensue because they simply had no shared reality with that geography, or the next question would be, "Were you in the oil/energy business?" to which we had to respond with a hearty, "Yes, we worked for the company that puts approximately 10 percent of the gas in your tank." That, too, often ended the conversation, because although everyone drives, we found ourselves deep in the heart of environmental activist land, and an assumption was made that if you are one thing, you must not be the other. Which is not reality.

This was the land where people climbed trees that were due to be felled and lived in them for years in order to save them. An instant set of assumptions landed smack in the middle of our conversations, and there was little welcome or invitation to progress any further. People's eyes would glaze over if I ever launched into a story about living overseas.

I learned quickly that what seemed like invitations to share some piece of information about my previous life was merely superficial politeness and not authentic curiosity. Because I have a certain worldview and people would ask how certain situations applied to Saudi Arabia, I believed they were truly interested; however, I quickly came to understand that few people in the US could carry on a conversation about another geographical place. Almost immediately I discovered that my Saudi experiences were untranslatable. People looked away. We become lost in translation not only in language but by our experience and sense of relevance.

MISSING "HOME"

Part of the process of return, as I've experienced it, is finding myself missing things that once were foreign, just like I missed parts of my life back in the US before I went overseas. In Bellingham, we missed the pressure around prayer time and shopping. My eyes longed for the sight of men wearing perfectly laundered white thobes with slung-back red and white ghutras.

When I moved from Japan to Saudi, I missed the millions of people in Japan, the pace of life, traveling by train, the biweekly colorful celebrations the Japanese live by. I missed the stimulation, the smells, tastes and pace of living. In Arabia, I spent the first five years missing driving. Returning home meant that I missed having a driver. Oh, how I longed for a driver to negotiate the ten-lane Interstate 5 in Los Angeles or the Katy Freeway in Houston for me. Other adjustments were called for, including the purchase of a light to lift my mood when awaking to the green, dark, rainy days in Bellingham.

I missed the proximity to recreation that Aramco had provided. I missed my houseboy. I missed not only the services Bennie provided but also his quiet, orderly presence in my home. I missed him calling to me as he arrived and immediately checking the rooms for his daily activities. Even now, ten years later, I prefer to have company in the house, even if there is no interaction.

My eyes very much missed looking at the Arabic language on the shop signs. When I returned home, it was interesting to be able to read every last word on signs and billboards. Yet, I was conscious that part of my brain missed Arabic calligraphy. For fifteen years I had absorbed this text, rarely understanding it but always enjoying its presence and the natural beauty it impressed upon me.

I missed the sounds of the prayer call. The prayer call had acted like church bells for me. In fact, church bells could be heard ringing daily over at King Fahd University of Petroleum & Minerals in Dhahran. For several seasons, I attended a water-aerobics class in the pool on main camp, and every day at one o'clock the rather odd and out of place sound of church bells rang.

I desperately missed Middle Eastern magic ... though I had rarely considered it in that framework before. I missed my friends and Aramco family. Those people, who assembled together, were my United Nations, my world community—and where was that world now? These were people with whom I had an enormous shared experience, people I did not need to explain anything to, people who read between the lines, understood the codes and spoke the invisible language of expats.

What did fitting back in even mean? How could I balance my desire to be global but live as a local? If I wasn't an expat, what was I? Who was I in the process of becoming? A hidden immigrant? No identity seemed to fit.

"Normal" was completely unacceptable, boring and disenchanting. I longed for Al Khobar and its messy streets. I missed people taking a left across four lanes of traffic at a red light. There were few enchanting moments in Bellingham. The regular experience of being out of my comfort zone was missing a lot of the time.

If I was an expat in the past tense, who was I now?

WHAT IS ARRIVING WELL?

The honeymoon period when setting off on adventure fills us with potential, possibility and positivity. Our imaginations are infused with pictures of what we will love. Endorphins swamp our brains; we feel terrific. At journey's end a kind of mental and physical rebalancing occurs that allows us to move forward. The return stage is an opportunity to gather the stories and reflect on how they change into the invisible golden nuggets or lessons that we carry forward. Generally, journeys that are well-reflected on upon completion lend themselves to more meaningful journeys in the future.

Yet, what shall we carry forward and how will we carry these sacred gifts? Here is the big fat secret, the one no one tells you when you set off on a new adventure. It turns out that every adventure, expat assignment or travel experience has a vast unpredictable set of consequences built in. No one escapes the transformation or changes that are baked into the mosaic of international travel. Besides the outward and obvious consequences of having to rebuild your life in the next place, an entirely new experience or new way of being has been created inside your mind and heart.

I believe it's perfectly natural to have changed, but sometimes we are the last to understand how and why we have changed so thoroughly.

Chapter 15

REFLECTION, REUNIONS AND LIFESTYLES

STITCHED TOGETHER

WE LIVED IN PROXIMITY OF FRIENDS, colleagues and neighbors within a company culture 24-7, all rubbing and polishing each other like a collection of sea glass in a jar. Unique, shared experiences were constant and even now somewhat indescribable to others outside that sphere. We were a diverse, interconnected and purposeful community created to discover natural resources and deliver them to the globe.

From the moment we arrived at the rough and tumble Dhahran airport and were met by one of John's colleagues, until fifteen years later when our neighbors across the street poured us into the taxi waving us a gay goodbye for that final exit-only journey, we had the benefit of a loving, supportive and tight-knit community. It was a lifestyle full of structure. Returning home after years overseas can feel like a vacuum, almost that sense that one is circling space inside a spaceship, disconnected from normal life.

Extraordinary experiences are marvelous in the moment, but there is a lasting price to pay. Forever there is the possibility that they set you apart in regular, everyday life.

Is it any wonder then that so many of us who've been abroad with Aramco spend time, money and attention on maintaining our Aramco-family connections? Reunions of all sorts are planned around the globe, from Austin, Texas, to Karachi, Pakistan. In a recent survey, Aramco retirees expressed their desire for connection. The Arabic tradition of tribe was emphasized and lived out so well in Kingdom that we still consider ourselves part of another tribe, an Aramco tribe. We have moved to the far-flung corners of the globe, yet friendships flourish over decades and across continents. Structure is provided through platforms like Facebook, the Aramco Expats website and by the company's support of official reunions.

A formal reunion event, called a *hafla* reunion, is held in the US every two years and frequently in other countries. Official reunions have been held in Kingdom, as discussed in earlier chapters. We were fortunate enough to return in 2015 for one of these. The event program read like a week-long party, which is exactly what *hafla* means in Arabic. Trips were available to Shaybah—a one-million-barrel-per-day oil and gas production facility, the most remote of its kind deep in the Rub' al-Khali desert—and to Mada'in Saleh, a UNESCO world heritage site, both on the company plane. Returning to touch the physical mystery of the desert made me feel as if my life back then was much more magical or mystical than life in the West; however, that was an illusion since the day-in, day-out reality was not always full of novelty.

Until 2019, entering the Kingdom of Saudi Arabia has been a privilege granted to a select few. Leaving the Kingdom meant, for almost everyone, that they will never return to their once-upon-a-time home. To re-enter and rediscover life there again was like clambering through a keyhole in time, space and culture. I felt a sense of magic like Alice in *Through the Looking Glass*. The Saudi government has approved tourist visas so at long last people can return to the Kingdom. The sense of isolation and separation from a childhood spent there or from decades of many lives lived there, can now be healed.

A GUEST ONCE MORE

Entering the Kingdom from Bahrain for the reunion meant driving across the King Fahd Causeway. Getting fingerprinted at the immigration booth was another first, as I had always just sailed through the booths with a Saudi visa intact in my passport. At the gate to the compound we were met by a very organized Aramco Annuitants Reunion Committee person, who gave us our bags of swag, detailed programs and something to drink. It was a dull, over-cast day in March, with a bit of humidity in the air. The familiar compound seemed somehow flat and shabbier than I remembered. A friend had offered her home as our residence, and her husband, Rick, was the perfect host, lending us his older car and making our visit seamless; yes—just as if we had never left.

My heart was touched driving past our old homes. The first on Nomad Trail was just as we had left it in 2008, but the second on Lime Tree Circle looked sad and dilapidated. The driveway, patios and windows were encrusted with sand, and it looked like the lovely yard we had enjoyed hadn't seen a gardener in five years. A misshapen eucalyptus continued to hold down the fort in the far corner, but I found very few promptings or memories of the green, grassy oasis that we called home for five years.

Once more we were reminded that it's the people in our lives who make the difference. My biggest joy was watching people's faces light up when they saw us. Many wondered why they hadn't seen us around for a while—well, it had been more than four years since we left.

The Commissary complex had been expanded and extended. While visiting the new supermarket we ran into one of John's colleagues, someone he barely knew or remembered. John found himself enfolded in the arms of this huge Saudi with the traditional kisses on the cheek. He enjoyed so many individual reunions with colleagues, both Western and Saudi, all joy-filled and boisterous moments with much back-slapping. I was struck by the smiles of the Saudi people on this trip. While living there, I was conscious that these people had a natural reserve of pure spirited joy that rose up like a fountain when you interacted with them; this visit delivered even more smiles and a sense of their natural ease with life.

Bennie had been our gardener and then houseboy for about twelve years. During that period we had watched him move from being a single guy with no car who had to hitchhike around the camp to a responsible husband and father of three children who all attended the private Indian school. His wife, who was a nurse, had applied to practice in the US; however, she failed her English test three times, so they contented themselves by living in Al Khobar, building a family and a home as houseboy and nurse. Meeting Bennie, catching up on his kids, his progress through life and his delights, was such a joy. My heart was full and overflowing with gratitude for the wonderful, patient light he had provided in our home all those years.

We went out to the Hobby Farm and found our first horse, a flea-bitten gray Anglo-Arab with distinctive habits and mannerisms. Shaiboo (his name is based upon a funny Arabic cartoon about a quirky old man) stood quietly grazing in his stall. Everything seemed so normal with him. He was immediately interested in carrots and some grain from his food bin. He nuzzled up to both of us, and as a bunch of cellular memories flooded my body with dopamine, I felt like I had finally arrived back home. Being around Shaiboo and the horses had always instigated an experience of well-being. I was aware of a great internal healing as I wrapped my arms around his neck and held him. We had purchased Shaiboo for Lynsey when she was in fourth grade; fourteen years later, here he was. Three months after the reunion, Shaiboo passed away naturally. We believe he was by then between twenty-three and twenty-six years of age. That was a seminal moment for us, like a thread of love to an old life had been cut.

Our groom Layakath had become the senior statesman of the Hobby Farm. Although he was not a supervisor, he had many more years and experience under his belt, and it was delightful to see the difference. Maturity had settled on him like a comfortable blanket, and I realized how much I had missed his calm wisdom. Sunil, the cook at the Hobby Farm, greeted us with a wide, cheerful grin and smiling eyes, and his memory of our favorite dishes was a treat for the heart.

Miriam, a Saudi friend, recounted the tale of Saudi wedding season. She, her mother and her sisters were invited to so many weddings during May and June, they had to divide them to attend twelve or fourteen each! Miriam, of course, showed up with gifts for me and updates on the corporate goings-on in project management. We've connected since the reunion trip, and she has opened her second business in Al Khobar, runs a household with three active children and has been promoted several times within Aramco while completing her master's in the UAE. She reminded me how ambitious Saudi women are and how they are able to juggle all this with support, usually a driver, a maid and a husband.

One evening the company threw a welcome home party for the annuitants near Half Moon Bay at the Executive and Management Clubhouse. Tables were groaning with food; candles and all the Saudi traditions were celebrated. We were greeted by about a dozen traditionally dressed swordsmen bearing the quintessential Saudi offerings in any home: Saudi coffee in tiny cups and dates. The traditional photograph holding a falcon was taken. A phalanx of retired and current vice presidents welcomed us in their pristine white thobes. Walking along the beach by the gulf with traditional Arab music in the background brought back such visceral memories. The price for such a mystical evening was a few speeches by management touting Aramco's progress.

Change was visible—painful, sometimes even shocking. The

Golf Shack had been a small café-like building. The new, upgraded building was huge, light and airy, set on the hill overlooking the golf course and the air base runway. Yet, this great Mexican restaurant was missing tortilla chips for the salsa they served. People in the know showed up with their own chips–*how normal*, we thought.

Construction equipment was operating on the Perimeter Road amid recently built new homes on the compound. With oil prices tumbling from 2013 onward, Saudi Aramco was expanding into alternative ventures and accelerating personnel hiring after our departure. While the overall lifestyle was recognizable to us, individual parts were transforming before our eyes.

Change occurs at the micro and macro levels of places, and returning to a place we called home was both reassuring and challenging. We noticed the elements of life that had stayed the same, together with the parts that had changed dramatically.

A CHANGED PERSPECTIVE

Although it is now very natural and easy for me to feel at home almost anywhere, the commitment required to live in one place and "settle" is clearly not anything I've acquired. Home is never the ground, soil nor habitat except when I'm in Scotland. Being the "other" has become my natural habitat.

Living in Saudi Arabia was transformative for me. While it taught me some of the toughest lessons, it also carried wonderful moments again and again. The end of the Arabian journey did not mean the end of the life journey, since the metamorphosis after "exit only" has helped me be more active, to continue traveling and to lead a more expansive and diverse life. A life I never would have dreamed of thirty years ago.

The biggest discovery? I prefer and indeed seek out the multicultural lane. Ideas and creativity naturally seem to percolate within a cross-cultural or interfaith community. I also identify with and indeed long for the grace that resides within the heart of diversity. Perhaps a strong dose of heart is required for all peoples to get along. The feeling of a mini-United Nations living inside a corporate cultural bubble forever permeates my mind and heart. Living in a state of wonder is not only useful but necessary for a more adventurous life.

Departure frequently presents itself as a closed door, but once we walk across that threshold, a new vista or vision is open to us. Other choices and possibilities come clearly into view. As foreigners we were on display in a sense. This challenged us to be more graceful, tolerant and positive, to rise to heights I previously could never have imagined. I believe the gift is in bottling these gifts, or golden nuggets, and effectively sharing them in the next journey. International living surely offers an exceptional opportunity to become culturally mindful and intelligent.

Despite arriving with differing values, customs and traditions, we were for the most part tolerated and frequently made welcome in Saudi. I value the tolerance, the good humor and the hospitality extended to us personally and professionally. Ram Dass co-wrote a book entitled *Walking Each Other Home: Conversations on Loving and Dying*. I wonder what our world would be like if we treated each other as honored guests wherever we are. What values would we practice if we set a solid intention to simply live in peace and "walk each other home"? In the meantime we can walk with each other, witness each other's successes and struggles and launch each other into new ways of being.

Upon returning to Arabia in 2015 I reframed my time spent there. There is a saying: "It's hard to see the picture when you are the frame." Forever I am grateful for the pioneering spirit of the expatriate women who went first, who made greater sacrifices, faced greater adventures and paved a path for us contemporary women.

Finale

Certainly, travel is more than the seeing of sights, it is a change that goes on, deep and permanent, in the idea of living.

—Miriam Beard

Chapter 16

SOUKS AND SAND

THEIR SMILING FACES BEAM OUT FROM the pictures like beacons. Wide-eyed accomplishment, that look of having summited a mountain of grand proportions, radiates toward the viewer. The customary picture taken standing by the "Exit Saudi Arabia" sign somewhere in the desert signals the sense of "we did it."

The faces of Aramcons glowing with joy, pride and completion are reminders of the pinnacle called "exit only" that we can stand on briefly for a few days. The shipment is packed, and the packers have left with our dozens of boxes. Lives sorted and sealed with no sign of the messy days that went before. Everything taped up neat and tidy, all designed to burst out, overflowing, spilling over with abandon on the other side, like leaves that have been boxed up and, when opened, return to their normal volume.

Those exit-only days are consumed by bureaucratic completion activities. Car sale–check; house inspection–check; pet certificates procured from the vet–check. The enormity of the moment can't ever fully land. For many global families those days are filled with memories of those who have already left. Many children are born in Arabia at the Dhahran clinic. Their very existence is pinned on a map forever. Their lives unfolded like prayer flags furling in the breeze, lived on the sand surface of the globe. Blessed be.

NOW WHAT?

The dreams of moving overseas to make a life filled with success, joy and excitement are about to appear in the rearview mirror.

Travel has been credited with broadening the mind, and recently further research confirms this. William Maddux, assistant professor of organizational behavior at INSEAD, concludes that, "The relationship between living abroad and creativity [is] consistent across a number of creativity measures (including those measuring insight, association and generation)." Global families have also been studied for high tolerance for ambiguity and holding two opposing ideas simultaneously.

The question is, what will this group do next, with our minds full of prayer-time, Rub' al-Khali excursions and the rough and tumble of downtown Al Khobar? Are we prepared for a destiny where we fit in or stand out? Will our identities be relegated to wearing an invisibility cloak for the remainder of our lives? Or will we tell the stories that demonstrate how changed at depth we are?

There are so many different ways to live. We have seen them. We have lived with them. They are not a myth but a string of magical, mystical moments we have strung together one breath at a time, over years, if not decades. How could one possibly be unchanged by this?

Like the souks we used to play in, the lined and textured faces of the locals become worn into the fabric of our souls. We will never forget those old men in wrapped-around ghutras, faces deeply lined like crop circles carved into human form. Wisdom poured out of those old Saudi fellows. I especially recall the gatherings outside the souk in Dammam near where the bus stopped. Toothless, ancient yet incredibly human, they were a welcoming force. For the most part they were full of humor, tolerance, patience and graciousness. This is what I choose to remember, sandy moments that reside in the cracks of my mind.

So, how have my cumulative experiences in the Kingdom altered my perspective? In total, my dreams, hopes and aspirations for the future have changed radically. The opportunity to visit other countries, listen to many languages and observe the interconnectedness of the human race has been a profound process that has encouraged a sense of deep empathy for humankind. I seek a world in which we can dissolve a portion of our borders, sit and talk evenly, ask questions and acquaint each other with the appreciation we individually have for our respective cultures and perspectives.

I take delight in my Saudi Arabian pilgrimage almost every day. From afar, my Saudi friends continue to support each other through the deaths of family members, serious health challenges, weddings, births of new grandchildren and all kinds of loss. Living, working and playing alongside the same people built community and lent itself to seeing into each other's souls. This does not end when we leave the Kingdom behind; it just takes different forms. Many choose to never look back, to move forward fast and never reflect on the experience. I, however, have discovered depths to plumb and lessons to be learned that I seek to apply to my Western life.

In my vision, world cultural curiosity would become the norm rather than the exception. We would all be willing to take our own personal quantum leaps and gladly risk (or sacrifice) our outmoded ideas of how to live. This is a reality in action as demonstrated by the mini-United Nations already functioning and harmonizing as a society in the deserts of Saudi Arabia. Almost everyone I meet who has lived in KSA has enjoyed a similar experience of feeling privileged to have been part of this grand experiment.

Imagine a world where we treat each other as honored guests while on this same life's journey. Could we live up to this ideal? Abayas are not just for covering women in Arabia. In the West we have our own coping behaviors, or "mental abayas," that we use to create a veil of secrecy and insecurity and the illusion of separation. My vision is for all the tribes and nations of the world to sit and listen carefully to each other, break bread together, get curious about what's possible and learn from each other's stories.

With seven billion of us, yes, our perspectives are bound to differ, but celebrating our differences makes us grow together. As we move around the table, travel the world and become allies, let's permit the strangely foreign to become the lovingly familiar. Let curiosity be the beacon that wins the day. Let curiosity WIN.

I arrived in Saudi Arabia willing to discover its mysteries. I departed Saudi Arabia having been mesmerized by her people and customs and continuing to wonder about more of her mysteries.

Perhaps the secret lies within each of us. Is it possible that, as we discover the world and steep ourselves in foreign cultures, we are merely revealing the wonders of the human spirit? If so, may you take the journey and discover those interconnected places. Perhaps the key to joy and peace is to "Eat together, pray together and hold each other's babies" (SaltProject.org).

May your soul be happy, and may you journey joyfully.

Postscript

SINCE OUR DEPARTURE NINE LONG or short years ago, much has occurred to change the Kingdom of Saudi Arabia.

ON WOMEN AND CHANGE

I spoke to Ayesha Malik, the millennial photographer who captured the image of a Saudi woman driving that was on the cover of *Time* magazine in July 2018. She said, "You cannot keep a country from embracing what everyone else has. Superstores, massive parking lots and malls are one part of the equation, but freedom and equality are more important." With the advent of the internet Saudi cannot remain isolated.

There is evidence everywhere one looks of more interaction between men and women that would have been *haram* just ten years ago. In April 2019 Joy (who is still living in Kingdom) walked into a Starbucks in downtown Al Khobar through its one entrance. This is huge, as men and women up until now have been segregated in restaurants. Sexual harassment also was finally deemed a criminal offense by the government.

More women than men in KSA have emerged successfully from higher institutions of learning in the last ten years. The ambitiousness that so many women have nurtured for decades has awakened the country as a whole. Sarah Al Suhaimi was recently appointed to manage the Tadawul, the largest stock exchange in the Middle East, with a market capitalization of about $320 billion. In the Saudi Shoura Council, from no women in 2012, there are now 30 women making up twenty percent of the council.

YOUTH AND CHANGE

The younger generation is forcing the narrative forward in directions that provoke fear within the establishment hierarchy. Saudi Arabia is no different in that respect. For every little disconnect there is a tiny movement forward. Ayesha mentioned that she frequently encounters Saudi millennials who are more liberal, outgoing and free-spirited than she is.

Art communities are historically leaders of social change. In downtown Khobar you will now find graffiti on buildings, concerts in public spaces and women jogging without abayas.

Freedom is leaking out everywhere. People are hopeful yet sensitive to where the traditions and culture lie and are not naïve about the shortcomings of the current system. Change is happening in the mindsets of the people.

Another Saudi friend told me recently, "The glue that holds our

Kingdom together continues to be our strong family ties." I asked her what her dreams for her country were. She replied that with Mohammed bin Salman at the helm, the country is steering toward a brighter future. She articulated her sense of hopefulness: "All of our dreams are coming true. We are heading in the right direction in steady steps. My kids can now live a wonderful life."

ON POLITICS AND CHANGE

King Abdullah passed away in 2015, a new King was installed, and then-Prince Mohammed bin Salman (also known as MBS) maneuvered himself into power to be the new Crown Prince. MBS was born in 1985 and was ten years old when I arrived in Arabia. As the youngest defense minister in the world, he is the deputy prime minister and first in line to the throne. He is considered a rock star by a generation of young Saudis, and his photograph is on their desktops, cell phones and tablets.

MBS has said, "I fear that the day I die I am going to die without accomplishing what I have in my mind. Life is too short and a lot of things can happen, and I am really keen to see it with my own eyes—and that is why I am in a hurry." The younger generation in Saudi resonates with this sentiment. The other side of the story is that princes and ministers were rounded up at the beginning of his administration and presumably coerced to cooperate. The war in Yemen has created a human calamity of nightmarish proportions. The shocking murder of journalist Jamal Ahmad Khashoggi set the world aflame with judgment. Saudi Arabia's international image has been forever tarnished by the allegations that MBS was involved.

However, who wouldn't want to live in a vibrant society with a thriving economy and an ambitious plan? MBS's "Vision 2030" plan's goals are to reduce Saudi's dependence on oil, diversify its economy and develop health, education, infrastructure, recreation and tourism.

They have ten years to implement it. Who would not want a diversified economy and better health, education and infrastructure? It seems that Saudi deserves the same opportunities and benefits that almost all countries are striving for. What are the chances? Time will be the final judge. This period of upheaval and the eventual results will one day soon be history.

For now, I wish the Kingdom of Saudi Arabia and most especially its wonderful people the best of success in the future. I am better for having met you and am grateful for everything you taught me.

I Am From

I am from jet lag with heart lag and soul all thrown in.

I am from airplanes and airports with every type of transportation.

I am from the Arabian Gulf 1970s, 1995 to 2010.

I am from Shukran and Allah with alhamdil-allah.

I am from dunes, deserts and Dhahran.

I am from salukis and falcons with some oryx, oh my.

I am from Mada'in Saleh, Jeddah and Ras Tanura, aha.

I am from oil, natural gas and petrochemical byproducts today.

I am from derricks and platforms.

I am from drillers and roustabouts.

I am from exploration, facilities and project management.

I am from the camp, the compound and camels plus more.

I am from TCNs, TCKs and jargon galore.

I am from Mother Aramco, a true company wife for sure.

I am from culture, curiosity and where is my place?

I am from dark skies, the Milky Way, the moon out in space.

I am from abayas, no driving and man planet for sure.

I am from Islam and Allah, the Quran and mosques all around.

I am from prayer call and sand dunes with sabkha alongside.

I am from Shaybah, Ghawar with Saffaniyah oil fields at large.

I am from King Al Saud to King Abdullah then Salman.

I am from abayas and thobes that are never too tight.

I am from crystalline sand roses that grow out of sight.

I am from adventure, the Middle East and unusual names.

I am from "fi yawn min," al'ayam ...

I am from once upon a time.

I am happy; I am ultimately from the Camel Lane.

Resources and Suggested Reading

SOURCES IN THE TEXT:

Chapter 7: *"[P]eople are people everywhere you go … ."* Natasha Burge, "Scud Kids Remember," *Aramco Expats*, April 22, 2016, http://www.aramcoexpats.com/articles/scud-kids-remember/.

Chapter 8: *"Expats or global nomads are now a tribe of 258 million … ."* United Nations Department for Social and Economic Affairs, *2017 International Immigration Report: Highlights*, p. 4, https://www.un.org/en/development/desa/population/migration/publications/migrationreport/docs/MigrationReport2017_Highlights.pdf

Chapter 16: *"The relationship between living abroad and creativity . . . ."* William M. Maddux and Adam D. Galinsky, "Cultural Borders and Mental Barriers: The relationship between living abroad and creativity," *Journal of Personality and Social Psychology* 96, no. 5, May 2009: 1047.

Postscript: *"I fear that the day I die . . . ."* Mohammed bin Salman, quoted in "Mohammed bin Salman Explains Why He Is Always in a Hurry," *Al Arabiya English*, November 24, 2017, http://english.alarabiya.net/en/features/2017/11/24/Mohammad-bin-Salman-explains-why-he-is-always-in-a-hurry.

Additional Resources

Ahmed, Qanta A. *In the Land of Invisible Women: A Female Doctor's Journey in the Saudi Kingdom*. Naperville, IL: Sourcebooks, 2008.

Al-Naimi, Ali. *Out of the Desert: My Journey from Nomadic Bedouin to the Heart of Global Oil*. London: Penguin Random House, 2016.

Beattie, Melody. *Journey to the Heart: Daily Meditations on the Path to Freeing Your Soul*. San Fransico: HarperSanFrancisco, 1996.

Bradberry, Travis and Jean Greaves. *Emotional Intelligence 2.0*. San Diego: TalentSmart, 2009.

Bridges, William. *Transitions: Making Sense of Life's Changes*. Boston: Nicholas Brealey Publishing, 1996.

Brown, Brené. *Braving the Wilderness: The Quest for True Belonging and the Courage to Stand Alone*. New York: Random House, 2017.

————.*Rising Strong: The Reckoning. The Rumble. The Revolution.* New York: Spiegel & Grau, 2015.

Brubaker, Cate. *The Re-Entry Relaunch Roadmap: A Creative Workbook for Finding Happiness, Success and Your Next Global Adventure After Being Abroad.* Small Planet Studio, 2016.

Calloway-Thomas Carolyn. *Empathy in the Global World: An Intercultural Perspective.* Thousand Oaks, CA: Sage Publications Inc., 2010.

Chaplin, Melissa. *Returning Well: Your Guide to Thriving Back "Home" After Serving Cross-Culturally.* Newton Publishers, 2015.

Copeland, Anne P. and Marissa Lombardi. *In Their Own Voice: Intercultural Meaning in Everyday Stories.* Sulaymaniyah, Iraq: The Interchange Institute, 2011.

Digh, Patti. *The Geography of Loss: Embrace What Is, Honor What Was, Love What Will Be.* Charleston, SC: Skirt!, 2014.

Dumler, Elaine Gray. *The Road Home: Smoothing the Transition Back from Deployment.* Westminster, CO: Frankly Speaking Inc., 2009.

Föllmi, Danielle and Olivier Föllmi. *Devotions: Wisdom from the Cradle of Civilization.* New York: Abrams Books, 2008.

Gardner, Marilyn R. *Between Worlds: Essays on Culture and Belonging*. Doorlight Publications, 2014.

Gielan, Michelle. *Broadcasting Happiness: The Science of Igniting and Sustaining Positive Change*. Dallas: BenBella Books, Inc., 2015.

Hanson, Rick, and Richard Mendius. *Buddha's Brain: The Practical Neuroscience of Happiness, Love and Wisdom*. Oakland, CA: New Harbinger Publications, Inc., 2009.

Hendricks, Gay. *The Big Leap: Conquer Your Hidden Fear and Take Life to the Next Level*. New York: HarperCollins, 2009.

Heinzer, Jeanne A. *Living Your Best Life Abroad: Resources, Tips & Tools for Women Accompanying Their Partners on an International Move*. Summertime Publishing, 2009.

House, Karen Elliott. *On Saudi Arabia: Its People, Past, Religion, Fault Lines—and Future*. New York: Vintage Books, 2013.

Huntley, Karyl. *Real Life Rituals*. Spiritual Living Press, 2005.

Iyer, Pico. *The Art of Stillness: Adventures in Going Nowhere*. New York: TED Books, 2014.

———. *The Global Soul: Jet Lag, Shopping Malls and the Search for Home*. New York: Vintage Press, 2000.

Janssen, Linda A. *The Emotionally Resilient Expat: Engage, Adapt and Thrive Across Cultures.* Summertime Publishing, 2013.

Jungers, Frank. *The Caravan Goes On: How Aramco and Saudi Arabia Grew Up Together.* United Kingdom: Medina Publishing Limited, 2013.

Knell, Marion. *Burn-Up or Splash Down: Surviving the Culture Shock of Re-Entry.* Tyrone, GA: Authentic Publishing, 2006.

Lacey, Robert. *Kings, Clerics, Modernists, Terrorists and the Struggle for Saudi Arabia.* New York: Penguin Group (USA), Inc., 2010.

Lemieux, Diane and Anne Parker. *The Mobile Life: A New Approach to Moving Anywhere.* The Hague, The Netherlands: Xpat Media, 2013.

Lindahl, Kay. *The Sacred Art of Listening: Forty Reflections for Cultivating a Spiritual Practice.* Nashville: SkyLight Paths Publishing, 2002.

Lippman, Thomas W. *Inside the Mirage: America's Fragile Partnership with Saudi Arabia.* Boulder, CO: Westview Press, 2004.

Livermore, David. *The Cultural Intelligence Difference: Master the One Skill You Can't Do Without in Today's Global Economy.* New York: AMACOM, 2011.

Loehr, Jim and Tony Schwartz. *The Power of Full Engagement: Managing Power, Not Time, Is the Key to High Performance and Personal Renewal.* New York: The Free Press, 2005.

MacDonnell, Judy. *Houses of Sand: Memories of Saudi Arabia.* Self-published, CreateSpace, 2011.

McCarthy, Patti. *Cultural Chemistry: Simple Strategies for Bridging Cultural Gaps.* Self-published, Cultural Chemistry, 2016.

Middleton, Julie. *Cultural Intelligence: The Competitive Edge for Leaders Crossing Borders.* London: Bloomsbury Publishing, 2014.

Nydell, Margaret K. *Understanding Arabs: A Guide to Modern Times.* Yarmouth, ME: Intercultural Press, 2006.

Osland, Joyce Sautters. *The Adventure of Working Abroad: Hero Tales from the Global Frontier.* San Francisco: Jossey-Bass Publishers, 1995.

Pollock, David C., Ruth E. Van Reken and Michael V. Pollock. *Third Culture Kids: Growing Up Among Worlds,* Third Edition. Boston: Nicholas Brealey Publishing, 2017.

Rubino, Anna. *Queen of the Oil Club: The Intrepid Wanda Jablonski and the Power of Information.* Boston: Beacon Press, 2008.

Rugh, Andrea B. *Simple Gestures: A Cultural Journey into the Middle East.* Washington, D.C.: Potomac Books, 2009.

Ryan, M.J. *How to Survive Change … You Didn't Ask For: Bounce Back, Find Calm in Chaos and Reinvent Yourself.* San Francisco: Conari Press, 2014.

Singer, Michael A. *The Untethered Soul: The Journey Beyond Yourself.* Oakland, CA: New Harbinger Publications, Inc., 2007.

Snedeker, Rick. *3,001 Arabian Days: Growing Up in an American Oil Camp in Saudi Arabia (1953—1962) A Memoir.* New York: Station Square Media, 2018.

Stegner, Wallace. *Discovery: The Search for Arabian Oil.* Vista, CA: Selwa Press, 2007.

Storti, Craig. *Why Travel Matters: A Guide to the Life-Changing Effects of Travel.* Boston: Nicholas Brealey Publishing, 2018.

———. *The Art of Coming Home.* Boston: Nicholas Brealey Publishing, 1996.

Webb, Lisa, ed. *Once Upon an Expat: An Anthology.* Self-published, Canadian Expat Mom, 2016.

Wood, Graeme. *The Way of the Strangers: Encounters with the Islamic State.* New York: Random House, 2016.

Glossary

NOTE TO THE READER: the Arabic language is written right to left, and the characters are only consonants, with the vowel sounds represented by diacritical marks. There are many ways to spell Arabic words in English. I have listed the most common translations.

ATCK—Adult Third Culture Kid

Aasif—"Sorry"

Abaya—The black coat overgarment worn by Saudi women

Adhan—The call to prayer

Afwan—"You're welcome"

Agaal—The head rope or fan belt that holds the ghutra or men's head scarf in place

Ahlan—"Hello"

Ahlan wa sahlan—"Welcome"

Ain—A spring or a well of drinkable water

al-Hamdil-allah—"Thanks be to God (or Allah)"

Al'ayam—"These days" or "the old days"; a reference to any period of time

Amir—A leader of a tribe or a prince

As-Salaam-Alaikum—"Peace be upon you"

Baba—Dad or Daddy

Baksheesh—A tip, a bribe, or a small gift

Bedouin—Nomadic, pastoral desert people of the Arabian, Syrian, or Northern African deserts

Bi-khayr, al-Hamdil-allah—"I am fine, praise God"; the common response to greetings

Bisht—A heavy cloak often made of wool worn over the thobe, especially on chilly nights

Bismallah—"In the name of God"; a formal response

Boshiya or Ghatwa—A full black veil completely covering a women's face

CCK—Cross-cultural kid; This term is used to encompass all types of children who are raised within a multi-cultural environment regardless to their unique situations. Therefore the term CCK includes TCK as a sub-group to describe children who fit the unique circumstances of TCK

Dabb—A very large lizard that lives in the desert; some people eat the tail

Dahl—A cave or limestone sinkhole

Dhahul—A racing camel

Dhow—Traditional Middle Eastern sailing vessels

Dibdiba—A flat desert plain

Dikaka—Sand plains covered with knee-high hillocks that drift behind woody shrubs

Dua—The prayer or worship before fasts start or end

Eid Al Fitr—The feast that breaks a fast, Eid Al Fitr follows the month of Ramadan, and Eid Al Adha follows the Hajj pilgrimage

Empty Quarter—The English word for the Rub' al Khali, a vast empty desert

Expatriate/Expat—A person temporarily or permanently residing in a country other than their native land

Fi yawn min—"Once upon a time"

Ghatwa—Another word for the veil (boshiya, ghatwa and niqab)

Ghutra—A head scarf worn by men

Grand Mufti—A leading Islamic scholar

Gyrba—A water bag made from goat's hide

Habibi—"My love" (masculine gender)

Habibti—"My love" (feminine gender)

Hafla—Party or social gathering, usually over the course of multiple days. In the belly dancing world, the term is used to describe an event where students, professionals and members of the public come together in the name of belly dance

Halal—Anything permissible by Islamic law; can refer to behavior, food or objects

Hallas—Complete or finished; "the end"

Haram—Anything forbidden in accordance with Islamic law; can refer to food, behavior or objects

Hidden immigrant—An immigrant who looks, sounds and behaves like the natives of their adopted culture

Hijri (or Hijra)—A.H. is the calendar abbreviation meaning "anno hegirae" used to indicate that a time division falls within the Islamic era

Hilal—The crescent moon indicating the beginning of the holy month

Home country—The country the expatriate calls home

Host country—The country that is sustaining or hosting the expat or foreigner

Hummus—A dip made from chickpeas, olive oil, lemon juice, garlic and tahini

Inshallah—"If God (or Allah) wills"; Allah willing

Jebel/Jabal—A rocky hill or promontory

Kabaa—Great Mosque of Mecca

Keffiyeh/Kafiyah/Kaffiyeh—The traditional red and white or black and white head covering for men

Khallas—A word to mean finish, stop, end or enough

Lion Bars—A British chocolate bar made by Nestlé

MREs—Meals ready to eat (US military)

Maafi mushkila—"No problem"

Maasalama—"Goodbye"

Majlis—A reception or entertaining area for guests, usually with large, low sofas

Marhabah—"Hello" or "greetings"; literally "God is love"

Mhendis—A mechanical person or engineer

Minfadlik—"Please"

Miswak—Teeth-cleaning twig from a tree, an old-fashioned dental cleaning method

Monocultural—A person or society that practices traditions and language from one culture

Mukhtal—Crazy or wild

Multicultural—A person or persons familiar with or operating within multiple cultures

Multilingual—Functional in several different languages

Mutawa (plural: Mutaween)—The religious police in Saudi Arabia

Na'am—"Yes"

Niqab—The half- or full-face veil Saudi women wear

Oasis—An isolated or fertile place in the desert

On the economy—Outside the Aramco compound(s)

Qadi—An Islamic court judge

Qawah—Arabic coffee

Qoran/Koran—Islamic holy book

Ramadan—The Muslim month of fasting

Ramadan Khareem—"Have a generous Ramadan"

Ramadan Mubarak—Exchanged at the beginning and end of the Ramadan month; "Blessed Ramadan"

Re-entry—Returning to a community or culture one lived in previously

Remittances—A money transfer sent by a foreign worker to their home country

Repatriation—The return experience to one's native culture

Riyal/Rial—Saudi Arabian currency—currently fixed at 3.75 riyals per dollar

Sabkha—A salt flat covered by a sandy crust

Saudi champagne—A nonalcoholic substitute for champagne made with sparkling water, juice, mint and sliced fruit

Scimitar—A sword or saber with a curved blade

Shamal—A huge sandstorm that blows in suddenly and blankets everything with a fine coating of dust

Shariah law—Islamic law or Muslim law

Shisha—A traditional Middle Eastern water pipe

Shukran—"Thank you"

Suhur—The meal prior to dawn during the month of Ramadan

Souk/Suq—A marketplace or bazaar, often selling similar items

TCA—Third Culture Adult

TCK—Third Culture Kid—a child raised in a culture different from that of their parents

TCN—Third Country National

Tabbouli/Tabbouleh—A salad made of chopped parsley and tomatoes

Tarawih/Taraweeh—Community prayers offered every night during Ramadan

Thobe (Thaub)—A white cotton robe worn by men

Visa—The stamp or sticker in a passport that allows you legally to enter a country

Wadi—A valley or dry riverbed

Walaikum assalam—The common response to "hello"; "And peace be upon you"

Wasta—Influence

Yellah—"Hurry up; let's go"

Zakat—Charity given to persons in need at the end of Ramadan

About the Author

DOREEN CUMBERFORD is a Scottish author who has been living internationally for over four decades. Her curiosity and global perspective are put to work as she helps people create global-hearted lives filled with travel, purpose and vision.

Living as an expat in seven countries on four continents, she believes that travel and storytelling spark our hearts and activate change across divides. Her inspirational keynotes to individuals and organizations overflow with matter-of-fact strategies for building cultural intelligence.

Doreen speaks and teaches effectively about exactly what is required to master major geographic transitions when moving overseas for short- or long-term assignments. Currently, she and her husband are on a grand, five-year adventure while pet sitting and housesitting across the world.

To learn more about her keynotes and programs, please visit her website at **www.doreenmcumberford.com**.

Keep the conversation going!

 doreenmcumberford  RockYourReentry  HousesittingLane

.

Made in the USA
Columbia, SC
24 June 2020